ESSENTIAL PSYCHOLOGY

General Editor
Peter Herriot

D2

MOTIVATION

ESSENTIAL

A

1 An Introduction to Psychological Science/*David Legge*
2 Physiological Psychology/*John Blundell*
3 Learning and Reinforcement/*Steve Walker*
4 Perception and Information Processing/*Paul Barber and David Legge*
5 Information Processing and Skills/*David Legge and Paul Barber*
6 Human Memory/*Vernon Gregg*
7 Thinking and Language/*Judith Greene*
8 Experimental Design and Statistics/*Steve Miller*
9 First Experiments in Psychology/*John Gardiner and Zofia Kaminska*

B

1 Social Behaviour/*Kevin Wheldall*
2 Interpersonal and Group Behaviour/*Judy Gahagan*
3 Values, Attitudes and Behaviour/*Ben Reich and Christine Adcock*
4 Social Psychology of Organizations/*Frederick Glen*
5 Psychology and Social Structure/*Barry Stacey*

C

1 Growing and Changing/*Harry McGurk*
2 Cognitive Development/*Johanna Turner*
3 Growing Up in Society/*Tony Booth*
4 Culture's Influence on Behaviour/*Robert Serpell*
5 In and Out of School/*Joan Freeman*

D

1 The Person in Psychology/*John Radford and Richard Kirby*
2 Motivation/*Phil Evans*
3 Approaches to Personality Theory/*David Peck and David Whitlow*
4 Individual Differences/*Richard Kirby and John Radford*

E

1 Psychology and Work/ *D. R. Davies and V. J. Shackleton*
2 Selection and Assessment at Work/*Gilbert and Helen Jessup*
3 The Psychology of Training/*Robert Stammers and John Patrick*
4 Men and Machines/*Hywel Murrell*
5 Motivation at Work/*Hywel Murrell*

F

1 Need to Change?/*Fay Fransella*
2 The Psychology of Handicap/*Rosemary Shakespeare*
3 Theories and Therapies in Clinical Psychology/*Dougal MacKay*
4 Community Psychology/*Mike Bender*
5 Psychology and the Environment/*Terence Lee*
6 Consumer Psychology/*Alan Frost*
7 Images of Man/*John Shotter*
8 Radical Perspectives in Psychology/*Nick Heather*

PSYCHOLOGY

MOTIVATION

Phil Evans

Methuen

First published in 1975 by Methuen & Co Ltd
11 New Fetter Lane, London EC4P 4EE

Printed in Great Britain by
Richard Clay (The Chaucer Press), Ltd
Bungay, Suffolk

ISBN (hardback) 0 416 83150 8
ISBN (paperback) 0 416 83150 5

We are grateful to Grant McIntyre of Open Books Publishing Ltd for assistance in the preparation of this series

Contents

Editor's Introduction

Phil Evans provides a review of the area of motivation which shows how we have moved from a view of organisms as being pushed by drives or pulled by incentives. Ideas of learned drives based on biological needs have given way to theories which stress that it is the way we perceive ourselves and our environment which determines our behaviour. The outstanding feature of this book is the way in which the underlying relations between different theories are made clear.

Unit D is a crucial part of *Essential Psychology*. Many who are dissatisfied with all current models of man see the concept of man as an individual and social person as the best alternative. This is because it emphasizes the uniqueness of the experience of each individual and also the notion that he acts upon his environment in a purposeful way. The books in this unit all demonstrate how the basic assumptions of personality theory and research are changing. Instead of personality being described in terms of forces driving people from within or events manipulating them from without, individuals are now being described as persons each with his own way of construing reality.

Essential Psychology as a whole is designed to reflect this changing structure and function of psychology. The authors are both academics and professionals, and their aim has been to introduce the most important concepts in their areas to beginning students. They have tried to do so clearly, but have not attempted to conceal the fact that concepts that now appear central to their work may soon be peripheral. In other words, they have presented psychology as a developing set of views of man, not as a body of received truth. Readers are not intended to study the whole series in order to 'master the basics'. Rather, since different people may wish to use different theoretical frameworks for their own purposes, the series has been designed so that each title stands on its own. But it is possible that if the reader has read no psychology before, he will enjoy individual books more if he has read the introductions (A1, B1 etc.) to the units to which they belong. Readers of the units concerned with applications of psychology (E, F) may benefit from reading all the introductions.

A word about references in the text to the work of other writers – e.g. 'Smith (1974)'. These occur where the author feels he must acknowledge an important concept or some crucial evidence by name. The book or article referred to will be listed in the bibliography (which doubles as name index) at the back of the book. The reader is invited to consult these sources if he wishes to explore topics further.

We hope you enjoy psychology.

Peter Herriot

I
A background to the study of motivation

It is not too difficult to see why motivation has become one of the central areas of investigation for psychologists. The science of psychology is more often than not defined as the study of behaviour and experience. When we witness an instance of behaviour, we want to ask the question: why? Why is that man, who is standing on the street corner, looking up at that tall building, and why now have half a dozen passers-by joined him in his gazing activity? Or in the laboratory, why is that white rat turning a wheel, now jumping over a barrier, and now running through the white door rather than the black one? The essence of the enquiring mind is not simply to observe behaviour but to find reasons for it and explain it. But reasons can be given at many different levels, depending on who is in search of the explanation, and when he is going to be satisfied. To illustrate this never-ending regress of explanation, we have only to look at the verbal behaviour of a typical five-year-old, who responds to every suggested explanation with a further 'why' question until we are in realms of explanation which present difficulties even for the omniscient parent.

Obviously there must be an end called somewhere, and

this is achieved by the simple expedient of drawing rough boundaries for an area of enquiry. This is clearly seen in the field of motivation: psychologists may use purely psychological words such as 'motive' and 'purpose' in their explanatory schema; they might also find it useful to go to the limits of their discipline which border physiology and look at the physiological bases of motivation (see A2 of *Essential Psychology*); in other cases they may be interested in the border with sociology and look at the influence of society on the behaviour of the individual (see B1). But when all is said and done every psychologist has some idea, possibly difficult to define clearly, of what constitutes psychological explanation.

In order to open up and introduce the field of motivation, let us now look at how we in fact use motivational words and what their use implies in the way of explanation.

The use of motivational words and their implications

We have used three common motivational words so far: 'motive', 'purpose', and 'reason'. The words are not synonymous and we shall see that more clearly when we ask another very important question: *where* do we find explanations of behaviour? If the behaviour is human, we might well find the explanation with the person himself. We ask him the reason which lies behind his activity. In discovering the reason, we might feel this constitutes a sufficient explanation (see F7). Take the example given in the first paragraph of the man looking up at the tall building. When asked for an explanation of his behaviour, he might well reply that his intention is to play a rather well-known practical joke and get every passer-by gazing skyward with him. The discovery of his intention seems *reason* enough, and we require no further explanation, although we may well wonder whether he does this sort of thing often. Notice here, however, that the motivation is completely covert. No amount of observation would have yielded the correct explanation, although the absence of other explanations and our knowledge of the existence of this practical joke might lead our suspicions in the right direction. Now suppose that there were smoke billowing from the top storey of the building. We should not feel the necessity of asking the man the reason for his staring, rather we should ask him the reason for the smoke. Thus in the latter case we seem to be finding an explanation for his behaviour in the external environment. The explanation is completely overt. The word *reason* then seems to be wide in its scope. We can find reasons in many places.

Let us now return to the white rat in the laboratory. Since we are unable to ask the rat any searching questions, we simply carry on observing it. At the end of its numerous and bizarre activities, the rat finds a supply of sugar pellets and settles down to eat them. We assume that the rat was hungry and that the *purpose* of the animal in expending so much energy was to get to the food. We might, however, have some reservations about attributing such things as purposes to rats. But for the moment why not?

When we ask what motivates behaviour, we are interested at first in a broad spectrum of possible answers. At a very basic level, we may find that the environment itself is able to account fully for the behaviour in question. For example, if someone is forcibly pushed to the ground by an aggressor, we do not ask the unfortunate victim why he fell (unless we wish to gain a fully justified reputation for sarcasm). When we trip over a kerbstone, we have little to do with our subsequent fall, except perhaps to ensure that we do not land on our heads. And if someone did ask us why we tripped, what else can we mumble other than: because of the lurking kerbstone.

Fortunately most of our behaviour does not consist of

such involuntary responses to animate and inanimate assaults. It is when we start behaving as agents and initiators of action that real 'why' questions become appropriate. In answering such questions, we tend to use words which shift the locus of control away from the immediate environment and inside the person. We speak of *drives* and *instincts* or *purposes* and *intentions*. We eat because we are hungry and hunger is supposedly the drive which explains our eating behaviour. Men conduct wars because they have aggressive instincts. The purpose of my visiting the garage today was to realize my intention not to run out of petrol on my way to work. We use these words very freely and very commonly, but just how valid is their use? How much do they explain? These are questions which will be raised throughout the book.

So when it comes to initiated behaviour we see many motivational words which point *inside* the agent, but that does not mean all motivational words point in that direction. When organisms behave, apparently purposively, they achieve certain things in the environment – often concrete things like money, or sugar pellets. We talk about these things as *incentives*, *goals*, or *rewards*. And we accept the use of these words as explanations of motivational 'why' questions. Does this mean that internal constructs such as drives etc. are not primary in explanations of motivation? Well, not necessarily. After all, something can hardly be called an incentive unless it is in some sense wanted. 'Wants', of course, belong firmly in that first class of words – firmly inside the person. (Some readers, however, may already be asking whether the 'wants' themselves may not be explained by looking *outside* the person.)

We have now completed a quick perusal of some of the vocabulary of motivation. This makes possible a preview of some of the areas of debate which have existed and still do exist in the psychology of motivation, and which, in turn, are very much connected with the different shades of meaning which attend the use of these words. All these areas of debate are taken up in detail in later chapters of the book.

Mechanism versus cognition

When I say that I have chosen a course of action and give you a reason, you can accept that the reason motivated my choice. You can also, however, turn round and say that regardless of the reason I have given you, I would have chosen the way I did any way. It sounds a bit like the old free will versus determinism debate (see F1, F7) – and in a sense it is. However, one can also think of it in the following way. In the former case I ask you to accept that a reason can serve as an explanation. But reasons are complex things, which imply a thinking, knowing organism. It is quite possible to eschew such cognitive words as reason and use words which imply a mechanistic process where an organism behaves solely as the victim of forces acting upon it. One need not thereby deny that a man has reasons for behaving; one simply denies that such reasons have any relevance in determining his behaviour. On this view reasons, intentions, and things of that ilk, are at most *epiphenomena*, things independent of the determining process.

Because we are so used to ascribing such things as intentions to human beings, it is better to look at examples from animal behaviour if we want to see the real difference between a mechanistic and a cognitive approach to motivation. When a rat runs a maze for food in the goal box, do we say that the rat has any kind of knowledge of the final reward, and do we go on to say that such knowledge of future consequences determines in any way the behaviour that occurs in the maze? If we do say this then we are propounding a cognitive theory of motivation. If, however, we maintain that the rat's behaviour can be fully explained without reference to cognitive terms (such as knowledge or intention), but only to forces already acting within an otherwise inert body then we are advancing a mechanistic theory. What are these forces which do not imply cognition? We look back to our vocabulary and discover words such as 'drive' and 'instinct'. They have no connotation of cognition, as indeed is attested by the phrase 'blind instinct'. Psychologists have differed and still do differ in the matter of espousing cognitive or mechanistic theories. Ultimately the issue between them must be resolved on the basis of evidence. If the mechanistic theorists are to be believed then the higher-level explanations of cognitive theorists will have to be shown to be redundant. If the cognitive theorists are right, then they must show that the mechanistic theories are inadequate to deal with the evidence. This debate is relevant to the next issue too.

Push versus pull

When an object moves from A to B, the force can either come from A in which case we say the object is pushed, or from B, in which case it is pulled. We have already seen above that a mechanistic theory treats an animal's behaviour in much the same way as that of a machine. What kind of force, push or pull, is more acceptable to this kind of theorist? The answer is clearly seen in the motivational word 'drive' – we think immediately of a force which pushes us, or goads us into action, where we would otherwise be as inert as a billiard ball resting on a table. Our behaviour results from the drive as a billiard ball's behaviour results from the push of the cue. To go back to the rat in the maze: without the push of his hunger drive he would stay in the start box. But can we not also conceive that the animal is pulled towards the goal box by the incentive (food)? There seems, however, to be a problem here for the mechanistic theorist, for the incentive presumably has to be *known about* in order to exert an effect. This implies cognition. If cognition is not to be invoked, one must find a way of getting round the apparent difficulty of a future event in the goal box influencing the prior behaviour of running the maze.

Innate versus learned

In the vocabulary of motivational terms which we have so far used, one word stands out very obviously as connected with innate behaviour. That word is *instinct*. To the layman the word instinct is more likely to conjure up ideas about animal behaviour than human. If the word is used to explain the motivation of human behaviour, it is a good bet that it is being applied to irrational animal-like behaviour. The Sunday press is quite likely to invoke the 'aggression instinct' or the 'sex instinct' as good motivational coat-hangers to account for a mutilated corpse in the canal or pornographic pictures in the vicarage. For the psychologist, however, it is not such an easy job to say how much of our behaviour can be accounted for by innate motivational factors, and how much of motivation is a matter of learning. It is true that we have little say in whether we eat, drink, or sleep. But even these apparently primary biological drives are not without their learned components, as we shall see when we discuss them in a later chapter. There is also the additional question of how far our obviously learned motives can be traced back to more primary sources. Do we work for the incentive of money, for example, because of some chain of associations back to a primary hunger drive? The way in which individual human motives are acquired is a question which any theory of motivation must consider.

Conscious versus unconscious

Most people have heard of Freud (see D3), and most people are aware that one of his major contributions to psychology was to emphasize the importance of unconscious factors in determining our day to day behaviour. Such a view, of course, considerably expands the meaning of the words we have been using. When we have talked of intentions or motives, we have wanted, if the subject be human, to ask the person what these are. But, according to Freud, he might not know. We shall be treating Freudian theory and its contribution to the psychology of motivation in a later chapter.

Such, then, is an outline of the area with which we shall be dealing. But our survey of the psychology of motivation cannot be considered in a void. Many people before twentieth century psychologists have addressed themselves to the question of motivation and their thinking must be considered in this introductory chapter.

An historical perspective

Sections on historical perspective, the tracing of the history of ideas in any area, usually begin with the ancient Greeks (see F1, F7), and there seems no reason to depart from this tradition, but not first without a mention of anonymous men in our earliest antiquity. Probably as long as there have been men on this earth, they have felt the urge to provide some explanation of human behaviour, simply because human behaviour is so different from the other events perceived in the environment. The behaviour of inanimate objects, by comparison, tends to be easily explained. 'Things' don't do anything on their own. They are acted upon. Even animals seem to behave predictably. Human behaviour enters the picture as something rather bizarre and unpredictable. The easiest way to account for it was to credit men with something special: they were not just bodies or things like stones or trees; they had souls.

The philosophy that human beings have bodies and souls is known as the philosophy of dualism. Plato and Socrates were dualists. They believed men to be free agents who in possessing souls raised themselves above the level of mere animals. The system of ethics which Plato and Socrates espoused was based on men being able to choose the good and the beautiful. Dualism of body and soul was reflected in a dualism of qualities. Goodness and beauty resided inside things, but they were themselves also capable of an independent existence – there were such things as the ideals of goodness and beauty. According to these Greek philosophers behaviour was determined by either two things: passion or knowledge. Passion was shared with animals. Knowledge gained through the use of reason was peculiarly human, and the achievement of goodness was necessarily entailed by the exercise of knowledge. After obtaining knowledge it would be a redundant question for a Platonist to ask; but what should I do? This rationalism was present in other Greek thinkers too. Aristotle believed that the main aim of life was happiness rather than goodness. But like Socrates and Plato, he too believed that his aim was automatically realized by the use of reason and the acquisition of knowledge. Wisdom was happiness.

This dualism between body and soul was to continue into Christian thinking and dominate it for many centuries. It fitted the Christian ethic that there should be a soul capable of rational choice of the good, which competed with the body and its physical passions, shared with soul-less animals.

Any dominant tradition requires an antagonist, and the main antagonist in this case has been hedonism, or hedonistic theories of various types. The word 'hedonism' comes from the Greek word for 'pleasure'. It seems nowadays a fairly common-sense view that our actions are determined in the main by whether their consequences are pleasurable or painful, but surprisingly those early philosophies which are usually seen as the precursors of the hedonistic tradition are not at all deterministic. We have seen already that the main Greek tradition traceable to Plato and Aristotle emphasized the freedom of the human agent. It follows that they had little to say about the determinants of human conduct, since it was not determined. Early hedonistic doctrines, however, had just as little to say. In the classical world, Epicureanism (after the Greek philosopher Epicurus) held great sway for a time, and its followers believed that the pursuit of pleasure was the purpose of life. However, at no time did Epicurus deny free will. Man's conduct was not determined by pleasure; it was simply man's duty to pursue it. Nor, incidentally, did Epicurus have sensual pleasures in mind when he urged his doctrines on his followers. He often lived on bread and water, and looked disdainfully on mere physical comfort! In a way then, Epicureanism should be seen as a variant of the mainstream, rather than an early antagonist. The psychological aspect of hedonism did not really come to the forefront until the British empiricists. By psychological aspect I mean an empirical belief that we do as a matter of fact act according to some kind of pleasure principle – this opposed to a philosophical position which may merely exhort us to behave in a certain way.

Utilitarians, such as Bentham and John Stuart Mill, actually start with the view that human kind does in fact behave in such a manner as to seek and hopefully obtain pleasure, and the political message of the utilitarians is that a society should take note of this reality. Therefore, so their reasoning goes, the best society is bound to be that which creates the greatest happiness and thereby the greatest good for the greatest number. With psychological hedonism we are much closer to contemporary thinking, for without detracting from the richness and variety of human behaviour it allows us to conceive of it as to some extent lawful in obeying a very general guiding principle.

So far our discussion of historical perspective has limited itself to questions of philosophy, and that is natural since philosophy is one of psychology's parent disciplines. We now look to the other parent, in the shape of biological science.

It is well known that Darwin influenced everything and everyone. His impact on psychology was huge. Up till then it had been usual to treat psychological questions as extensions of philosophical ones, and no one had thought of leaving the philosopher's armchair, especially since the famous Immanuel Kant had already declared some time previously that psychology could never be a science. Yet with the growth of interest in ideas of evolution, it became first of all possible to surrender the belief that man was somehow special and separate from the other animals, and thus man himself became fair game for scientific observation and study. Secondly, the behaviour of man also became something which cried out for explanation. No longer was it enough to account for human actions by appealing to notions of free will and free agents. In the late nineteenth century science tended to become synonymous with a zealous belief in the supremacy of causation and determinism. If then, psychology were to be respectable and scientific, it had also to deal in causes and determinants. As far as the psychology of motivation is concerned, there is one figure who stands out as being most influenced by the Darwinian revolution in science. That man is Freud (see D3). Because Freud demands to be treated in more detail than can be given in a section on history we shall be returning to him later on, but we may mention here just two ways in which he was influenced. First, he was dogmatic determinist – nothing, but nothing, occurred without a cause. Second, in his search for the ultimate motivational causes of behaviour, Freud wished to ground his theories in the respectable domain of biology. In choosing the vicissitudes of the sex instinct to play the role of prime motivator he achieved his aim. His theory may have appeared extremely speculative, but it was thoroughly biological.

One consequence of the eradication of the separate status of man enjoyed before Darwinism was a growth of interest in studying animal behaviour. Instinctive behaviour patterns were noted in spiders and wasps, and gradually instinct became a concept which psychologists used in talking about human motivation. Apart from Freud, who put all of the emphasis on sex and aggression, there were psychologists such as William James and later McDougall, who credited human beings with many more instincts. Though agreeing that instincts in man were not as fixed or rigid as in the lower animals (both James and McDougall saw them as capable of being modified by learning) nevertheless discrete instincts were invoked in order to provide the motivation for a number of diverse human activities. Thus playing, washing, or even just being sociable were behaviours underpinned by their respective instincts.

It is difficult nowadays to read, say, McDougall without thinking that his proliferation of instincts explains just about everything and nothing. What instinct, I wonder, is activated when I listen, as I have just done, to a violin concerto? And is it a different one from when I listen to a piano concerto, or a symphony? Nonetheless we must remember that in those days McDougall was reacting against a philosophical psychology in favour of a biologically based science. For that reason alone the concept of instinct must have been an attractive one. Soon, however, that concept was to go into decline.

The decline happened in the first decades of this century when a psychologist, J. B. Watson, enunciated the tenets of behaviourism. The behaviourists as their name implies, thought that psychology ought only to concern itself with what was observable. What was observable in the field of psychology was simply behaviour. Thus methods of investigation relying on introspecting such things as mental events were banished from the arena of respectable scientific procedure. However the behaviourist movement was also enamoured with the principles of conditioning (i.e. the chaining of simple responses to simple stimuli) which were currently being investigated. It became something of a behaviourist article of faith to deny innate factors in the explanation of behaviour. The variety of human activity could all be explained by different conditioning experiences. Since instinct implied innately laid down propensities to action the word rapidly became unfashionable and was banished to the wilderness for some time.

To take this historical review past the behaviourists would be to pre-empt much of the material of later chapters. With the behaviourists we move out of the area of history and into the field of the contemporary or near contemporary.

Guide to subsequent chapters

It will be clear by now that no account of motivation is complete unless it takes into consideration the basic truth that we are biological organisms (see A2). Accordingly the next two chapters will be concerned with looking at the biological basis of motivation in animals and man. Chapter 2 examines the current status of instinct in the psychology of motivation. Chapter 3 is devoted to a survey of the motivational mechanisms underlying such primary biological behaviour as eating, drinking, sexual activity, and sleep. Chapter 4 will move on to a more general analysis of behaviour, which will aim to show how a mechanistic drive theory has been used in attempts to explain the whole gamut of purposive behaviour in both animals and men. The exposure of the weaknesses of drive theory will lead us into a consideration of more cognitive approaches to the question of motivation – that will make up Chapter 5. Chapter 6 will start off by considering the contribution of Freud to the study of motivation. However, Freud's system of psychoanalysis did not stand still during his lifetime, nor afterwards. We shall assess the revisions of later psychoanalytic thinkers, particularly existential thinkers and their very contemporary brethren – the humanistic psychologists. The final chapter, like most final chapters, will attempt the eclectic and thankless task of integration.

Summary

1 The question of motivation is the question 'why' asked in the context of behaviour. Such questions can be asked indefinitely and we limit the scope of our answers to what we roughly delineate as the discipline of psychology. We do find some answers straddle the sister disciplines of biology and sociology, because man is fundamentally a biological organism and a social entity.
2 Motivational answers use motivational words. The use of these words has implications particularly when it comes to considering *where* we find acceptable answers.
3 The fact that some words imply cognition and others do not, the fact that some words look for answers inside the organism whilst others look outside – these facts sketch the very controversies which psychologists debate.
4 The present approach to motivation became possible when philosophical thinking moved away from questions about how man ought to behave given free will, to questions about how man does in fact behave, leaving the

question of free will aside. The Darwinian revolution also encouraged the view that man's behaviour was not something sacrosanct but open like all other phenomena to scientific observation.

2
Instinct

Organisms of all kinds engage in what seems to be purposive behaviour – they appear to seek and obtain clear goals in their environment. To ask what motivates such behaviour is, in terms of getting an adequate answer, to ask what factors control it. We have seen in the last chapter that early psychologists, such as McDougall, reacting against their philosophical heritage and eager to 'biologize' psychology, utilized the concept of instinct in their discussion of motivation. Instincts were seen as primary sources of energy which were responsible for guiding all sorts of activity. But we may remember that instinct soon went out of fashion as an explanatory concept with the rise of behaviourism and its attendant and strident environmentalism. During the 'twenties and 'thirties instinct was all but dead – certainly amongst psychology academics.

Nevertheless instinct survived, not least because of the creative work of a group of scientists who, part zoologist and (smaller) part psychologist, carried out observations of naturally occurring animal behaviour. Their science generally goes under the name of ethology. Despite earlier roots, the word 'ethology' has now come to mean the study of animal behaviour, often but not always in a natural setting. When the science is extended to the study of human beings it is usual to prefix it: human ethology. The two most outstanding ethologists, in the early days of research, have been Konrad Lorenz and Niko Tinbergen.

Instinct, according to these writers, is an inherited stereotyped sequence of activities, which has its own particular energy. Put in rather simpler language, we envisage behaviour which, however complex it might appear and however purposive it might be, is nevertheless innately built into the animal and is not shaped by learning experiences; because of this it is rather fixed and rather rigid. The behaviour associated with a particular instinct is said to be *released* by certain quite specific evironmental stimuli or configurations of stimuli. Let us see now how this proposition applies to an instance of animal behaviour which has become quite traditional in the ethological literature of the day.

In a comprehensive study of the male stickleback (*Gasterosteus* – a fresh-water fish dear to the hearts of foraging boys with jam jars) Tinbergen conceived the idea of a hierarchical organization of instinctive patterns of behaviour. The major instinct, for the purposes of this example, was the reproductive instinct. Immediately below in the hierarchy, one finds a subordinate aspect of the instinct which we can call the mating instinct. This in turn could be subdivided into a variety of smaller sequential behaviour patterns such as zig-zag dancing leading to the female in the nest, fertilizing the eggs, and so on. Of course the whole mechanism has to be driven, and the major instinct itself is assigned what is supposedly its own specific *reaction energy*. Neural centres inside the animal's nervous system are posited as the reservoirs for this energy and these neural centres are themselves arranged hierarchically. When a specific stimulus comes along the appropriate neural centres are activated and the related behaviour is released. Thus one envisages a series of innately determined mechanisms which release behaviour – not surprisingly they have been termed *innate releasing mechanisms* (IRMs).

Various real-life patterns of behaviour are more eloquently described in the words of Tinbergen (1951) himself:

In spring, the gradual increase in length of day brings the males into a condition of increased reproductive motivation, which drives them to migrate into shallow fresh water. Here, as we have seen, a rise in temperature together with a visual stimulus situation received from suitable territory, releases the reproductive pattern as a whole. The male settles on the territory, its erythrophores expand, it reacts to strangers by fighting, and starts to build a nest. Now, whereas both nest-building and fighting depend on activation of the reproductive drive as a whole, no observer can predict which of the two patterns will be shown at any given moment. Fighting, for instance, has to be released by a specific stimulus, viz. 'red male intruding into the territory'. Building is not released by this stimulus situation but depends on other stimuli. Thus these two activities, though both depend on activation of the reproductive drive as a whole, are also dependent on additional (external) factors. The influence of these external factors is, however, restricted; they act upon either fighting or buildings, not on the reproductive drive as a whole.

But not all sequences of behaviour which occur in the satisfaction of an instinct are entirely mechanical. Tinbergen (1951) makes an important distinction between *appetitive activity*, associated with the search for a goal, and *consummatory activity*, which consists of those sequences of responses which are made when the goal is reached. Consummatory activity, he says, is relatively simple and takes the form of a fixed chain of responses.

Appetitive behaviour, on the other hand, allows for a whole variety of responses from the mere reflexive, through primitively learned reactions to what could be described as insightful behaviour. To elucidate this distinction between appetitive and consummatory activity, Tinbergen instances the hunting behaviour of the peregrine falcon. Random searching of a wide area leads to the spotting of a potential prey. Depending on the nature of the prey (a sick gull, perhaps, or a running mouse) the falcon will initiate a strategy for catching its victim, but this is still not consummatory behaviour, though it is appetitive activity of a more restricted kind. Only when the prey is finally caught is the chain of consummatory behaviour enacted.

Tinbergen considers that this kind of analysis has great heuristic value across a broad spectrum of animal behaviour: purposeful appetitive behaviour endowed with much plasticity, leads to the release finally of fixed consummatory patterns of activity.

We have noted that a specific reaction energy has been suggested as the motive power in various instincts. There is however one sort of observation which apparently seems to run counter to this notion. Picture this scene. Two cock birds are busy having a rather bloody fight. Suddenly one of them leaves off from the fray and begins to peck the ground, a response clearly not in the repertoire of fighting behaviour. Why is it then that an animal which is obviously under the drive of one particular instinct, will in some cases suddenly exhibit behaviour characteristic of another instinct? First, we may notice that such paradoxical behaviour occurs most often in situations involving conflict. It is almost as if a suitable response is momentarily blocked but the supposed instinctual energy is still being pumped up. The result is that a *displacement* from an obvious to a non-obvious response occurs. In fact the kind of behaviour we have mentioned is known as *displacement activity*. Not all behaviour can serve as displacement activity.

Relatively pure reactions which are known to occur as specific instinctual responses to specific stimuli tend not to be utilized as displacement activity. Less specific activities, on the other hand, such as general foraging movements in birds, or elements of nest-building behaviour, are used quite often. Tinbergen also points out that displacement activity is seen most often in situations involving either hostility or sexuality. This is not altogether surprising since we should expect just such situations as these to contain a greater degree of potential conflict.

We began this discussion of displacement activity by being made aware of a certain contradiction between (a) the idea that different instincts have their own instinctual energies, and (b) that energy subserving a thwarted instinct could lead to the triggering of alien activity. But the contradiction is not really so clearcut. If it were just a case of energy being thwarted in one respect, finding an outlet in another, then we should expect the displacement activity to be clearly and competently executed. Yet one of the main observations in this area is that the displacement activity is often incomplete and bizarre in its approximation to the normal form. Tinbergen has suggested that this may be due to the fact that the inhibition of mutually antagonistic drives, which often sets the scene for such behaviour, also ties up a lot of the energy, preventing full and proper release of any behaviour at all. Certainly the exact nature of displacement activity is very far from being a settled question, and it would be wrong to leave the reader with the impression that everyone agrees that a displacement of energy is involved. The observations of the ethologists are not in doubt. But the energy interpretation may not be the best explanation. For instance it is perfectly possible to see some displacement activity, if not all, as responses which, because of past appetitive associations, are able to diminish the anxiety, which we may presume to follow the frustration of an instinct.

We have so far laid great stress on the role that certain perceived stimuli have in the release of instinctive patterns of behaviour. However, Lorenz (1950) has drawn attention to instances of instinctive behaviour where complete sequences of activity take place in the absence of any observable releasing stimuli. Such behaviour has been labelled *vacuum activity*. Lorenz's view is that energy builds up rather like water in a reservoir. When the reservoir gets too full it will release its energy with or without the usually required sign stimuli. As with displacement activity there is no compelling reason to accept this interpretation based on energy flow. It is quite possible to argue that the thresholds for the elicitation of the behaviour in question are gradually lowered with time, such that a very minimal level of stimulation approximating only remotely to the ideal sign stimulus is enough to trigger the instinctual chain of responses.

To be fair, Lorenz's model does take account of the quality of releasing stimuli. He assumes the probability of certain activities to be a function of both the strength of releasing stimuli and the quantity of accumulated energy. If the energy reaches a high enough level, discharge into behaviour will occur spontaneously. Conversely, when the amount of energy is low, activity will only be triggered by very strong releasing stimulation. Thus we see not a fixed threshold but a changing one, which responds to the state of balance existing among the following interdependent factors: the amount of specific energy, the adequacy of releasing stimuli present, the frequency with which the activity has been elicited, and the rate at which energy accumulates.

It seems all very well to note how much animal behaviour is fairly stereotypically elicited by releasing stimuli affectting innate mechanisms, but human behaviour might be thought to be beyond such simplicity. Not so, according to the ethologists. For example, human parental responses, assumed by Lorenz and Tinbergen to be instinctual, are released by very specific sign stimuli: the baby must have, as all babies fortunately do have, a short face in relation to a large forehead, protruding cheeks, and maladjusted limb movements. Lorenz argues that the power of these sign stimuli is seen in their exaggerated use in the manufacture of dolls, in the portrayal of cartoon characters, and last but not least in the selection of our pets. Ethologists have also shown fixed responses in babies to various specific stimuli. Smiling is released by specific facial configurations; sucking by tactile stimulation to the cheek (see Bowlby, 1969).

Despite the paucity of hard evidence and the obvious scope for analogous speculation, ethologists from the academic pages of Lorenz and Tinbergen to the more popular pages of Desmond Morris have never doubted the breadth of instinctive behaviour in man. Thus a man's pensive stroking of his chin becomes displacement activity, involving an instinct of creature comfort going back to the pre-shaving dawn of mankind, whilst womankind in conflict pats her already perfectly arranged head of hair. What we do with our cigarettes in the service of the sex instinct is nobody's business.

Perhaps we should conclude here that the difficulty for ethologists in this area is to agree on a list of human instincts and to convince others by hard evidence that the list is correct. And yet no one can afford to be too skeptical of the existence of a number of relatively fixed action patterns in man, and it will be of great interest and importance to search them out and investigate them. In so far as man is a biologically-evolved organism, it would be reckless in the extreme to deny him the possession of instincts.

Criticisms of the ethological position

The major focus of attack for those not committed to a Lorenz–Tinbergen orientation has been the primacy given by these authors to the concept of instinct itself. Although ethologists generally have become more and more willing to admit the importance of environmental factors in the modification of behaviour patterns, it has always been a major part of their thinking that one should begin with a study of the instinct, and only bring in learning at a later stage. However, the shaping power of the environment cannot be so easily relegated, since it affects not only the directional behaviour of the developing organism but can also sometimes affect the structure. For example, the temperature environment of the fruit fly larva has a direct effect on the number of legs which will develop. Early learning experiences, including prenatal ones, are not without their effects on what are subsequently labelled 'instinctive' patterns of behaviour. The force of this argument is not at all to deny innate factors in behaviour; it is to cast doubt on the utility of beginning one's classification of behaviour with the term instinct, since the upshot of its usage might well be to obscure a really much more complicated picture. The use of the word 'instinct', in other words, serves to bind and constrain research. The trouble with first 'seeing' the instinct, and then observing the relevant behaviour can be that one's interpretation of events is not necessarily going to be the most parsimonious (see A1). Let us look at a specific example of this criticism in operation.

One of the classic series of experiments performed by Lorenz and Tinbergen in the late 'thirties involved constructing out of cardboard a number of silhouettes of bird shapes which the experimenters then passed over cages of geese. Whilst doing this, they recorded the degree of alarm response elicited by the models. They found that the most effective alarm raiser was any silhouette with a short neck, characteristic of a bird of prey. One particular silhouette (see Fig. 2.1) proved particularly effective in so

Fig. 2.1 *The hawk-goose silhouette* (*after Tinbergen, 1951*)

far as it elicited an alarm response only when it was flown from left to right, i.e. so as to resemble a short-necked bird such as a hawk. When the model was flown right to left, giving the appearance of a long-necked bird such as a goose, no alarm responses came from the enclosure.

According to Lorenz and Tinbergen this experiment demonstrated an innate releasing mechanism especially adapted in the course of evolution to a certain feature of birds of prey. However, critics such as Schneirla (1965) have pointed out that the explanation of this finding could be far more general. He points out that all organisms tend to withdraw from any source of stimulation which is both strong and sudden in its onset. Schneirla suggests that Lorenz and Tinbergen would have got a similar result if they had used a plain triangle as a model. Drawn base first across the field of vision it would have provided sudden stimulation, whereas vice versa the stimulation would have increased gradually. Another possible criticism of the first experiment was that the geese were not fully naive and could well have learned to recognize hawk shapes. Green *et al.* (1966, 1968) have since replicated and extended the research and shown the effect with naive ducklings. They also tested Schneirla's predictions about a triangle model but failed to confirm it. The original research therefore stands supported in this instance. However, critics such as Schneirla have been immensely valuable in showing the need to be cautious about fitting supportive findings too quickly into one's theory. Also a successful replication of Lorenz's and Tinbergen's work does not in any way get over the conceptual difficulties inherent in such terms as 'innate releasing mechanisms'. If one had to give a simple summary of what was wrong with this term the answer is to be found in the words themselves. First, the word 'innate' can too easily beg the question and perhaps incorrectly lead to a neglect of other factors in their development. Secondly, the word 'releasing' implies that the stimulus in question merely has the property of releasing a ready response. But perhaps that stimulus has other important functions like arousing or orienting the animal. Lastly, the word 'mechanism' implies just one triggering switch which is centrally placed. It has been suggested that this clouds rather than illuminates that very important area of research into the way stimuli are *filtered* in the nervous system (see A4). It is evident that all animals are selective in the sensory information which is available to them in the environment. It is thus an important question to ask where the ignored stimuli are filtered off from the so called sign stimuli which control behaviour.

We have already seen that the original model of Lorenz was an energy model. In fact its best description is a psycho-hydraulic model. Energy, more or less specific to an instinct, builds up in hypothetical reservoirs and is discharged as a function of both the presence of the right sign-stimuli and the amount of accumulated energy. A rough representation of the model can be seen in Figure 2.2. Here the tap represents the source of instinctual energy. A reservoir stores it. Energy is released into the trough (behaviours) by the force of energy in the reservoir, and the pull exerted by the 'weight' of external sign-stimuli.

The psycho-hydraulic model has been sharply and widely criticized. First on the grounds that such a model is far removed from what we know of the functioning of the nervous system. Perhaps, though, this blanket criticism is a little unfair since a behavioural model does not necessarily aim to mirror the functioning of the nervous system. Far more relevant are criticisms that the psycho-hydraulic model just does not fit the facts. It can be seen that in Lorenz's model energy can only be released through the

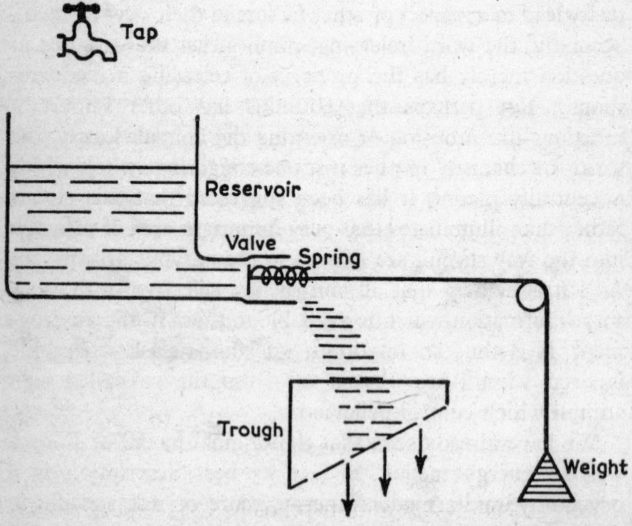

Fig. 2.2 *Lorenz's psycho-hydraulic model (after Lorenz, 1950)*

performance of instinct-related behaviour. If this were the case we should expect that consummatory behaviour (activity associated with the final goal: the obvious example is eating) cannot be bypassed. And yet we find there are a number of instances where consummatory behaviour is bypassed. Animals deprived of food, and therefore accumulating reaction energy, can be fed directly into the stomach, bypassing consummatory eating by means of a fistula. According to a Lorenzian model, the animal should nevertheless commence eating if given the opportunity. This is not in fact the case. It seems that signals of the arrival of food are received centrally, and hunger motivation is turned off (see Ch. 3). It might be argued that the psycho-hydraulic model applies much more to patterns of behaviour other than hunger and thirst; but even the reproductive behaviour of the much-researched male stickleback appears to contradict in some respects the predictions of the model. Male sticklebacks appear to reduce their hypothesized accumulation of energy simply by being allowed to view the newly laid eggs of the female; it does not seem necessary for the male stickleback to fertilize them in the service of instinct.

It is clear that there is now no longer any universally accepted ethological behaviour. It is also clear that the area is wide open for future fruitful research. Nevertheless it is at least possible to declare that instinct is not yet dead as a concept. The reader interested in exploring this area in greater detail, especially the various criticisms which have been ranged against the classic formulations of Lorenz and Tinbergen, are recommended to read Hinde (1970).

Summary

1 Instinct, as a concept in psychology, was kept alive during its period of demise by the ethologists, notably

Lorenz and Tinbergen. They were responsible for many ingenious experiments and observations relating to fixed behaviour patterns in animals, seemingly released by specific sign stimuli.

2 The notion of innate releasing mechanisms is criticized on the grounds that it begs the question of innateness too quickly, it ignores other functions the stimulus might have other than releasing ones, and finally, its positing of one mechanism obscures the intriguing question of how the stimuli are filtered from periphery to centre.

3 The hydraulic model of Lorenz is also criticized as being too rigid to explain all observations, apart from the side issue that hydraulic models are not appropriate since they do not reflect nervous system functioning.

4 The behavioural observations of ethologists remain valid and useful, nevertheless.

3
Physiological aspects of motivation

In this chapter it is intended to discuss certain kinds of behaviour in which the motivation is intrinsically related to physiological functioning (see A2). Such behaviour includes eating, drinking, sleeping, and sexual behaviour. The work that has been done on eating and drinking is particularly relevant as an introduction to the subsequent chapter on motivation and its role in learned behaviour, since experiments in animal learning have most commonly used laboratory rats motivated by deprivation of food and water.

Hunger

Hunger motivation has two aspects. It is both *general* and *specific*. Any organism requires a certain minimum of general food-stuffs in order to prevent it from starving to death; when its supplies are depleted the animal will search around until it finds food – such is the nature of general hunger. However, animals also require different kinds of food in order to satisfy specific hungers related to specific physiological needs. The physiological investigations of hunger have taken account of both the general and specific aspect. It is general hunger that we discuss first.

It is generally true that animals have the extraordinary ability to regulate very finely their intake of food against their expenditure of energy. Such exceptions as there are tend to be found in the human species of the so called advanced societies. Over lengthy periods most animals will maintain a constant body weight. If the need for more food is dictated by greater physical exertion or colder climatic conditions, then the animal will eat just enough to meet these changes of routine. The important question to ask then is what lies behind this ability to regulate eating. What factors control general hunger?

We are all well aware of the physical signs which accompany a long break between meals. Our stomachs begin, sometimes embarrassingly, to rumble. The most popular early theory was that stomach contractions were the physiological basis of hunger. Unfortunately this simple and attractive theory is quite easily discredited as a total explanation of hunger, since it has been shown that gastrectomized animals (i.e. animals which have had their stomachs surgically removed) are nevertheless quite capable of controlling their eating. Instead of eating normal 'meals', such animals eat a lesser quantity of food at more frequent intervals. The idea that the stomach, even when present, is the crucial source of hunger signals to the brain is convincingly refuted by Grossman and his colleagues (1947). They severed the nerves running from the stomach to the brain, thus cutting off all sources of neural information between them. Nevertheless the animals so treated soon recovered and continued to be proficient feeders.

Note, however, that these findings do not rule out the possibility that the stomach may, in normal animals, play some role in controlling eating. What is ruled out is that it is a necessary and sufficient condition of hunger regulation. To some psychologists of an earlier age this was not at all a surprising discovery, for they never expected the control of hunger to be a peripheral matter. Rather they believed that a hunger mechanism, if it existed at all as a single entity, would lie centrally: that is, in the brain itself. Although the findings reported so far do not prove this (there might, for example, be other peripheral control centres such as the duodenum whose contractions might signal hunger) they certainly seem to support a central theory.

The role of the hypothalamus

The hypothalamus is a small but vitally important area of the brain. Reference to any text dealing in neuroanatomy (see A2) will show that the hypothalamus forms the floor of the posterior part of the forebrain, which is called the diencephalon. The hypothalamus, as its name implies, is situated below the thalamus. One might easily guess at the importance of this area of the brain by observing how many neural tracts enter it and leave it, making their way to and from the cerebral cortex as well as the more posterior portions of the brain. The hypothalamus is also directly connected to the pituitary gland by means of the pituitary stalk. All these factors mean that the hypothalamus is uniquely suited to the measurement of metabolic changes and the initiation of rectifying activities. In terms of hunger, this means that the hypothalamus might well be the key to the discovery of a central mechanism which switches feeding behaviour on and off. Let us now look at evidence which has accumulated in support of this speculation.

With the advent of stereotaxic techniques for electrode implantation (such techniques involve rigid clamping of the head such that very exact placements can be made), it became possible to investigate nerve activity in very small areas of the brain. Tissue could be surgically destroyed, i.e. ablated; alternatively, cells in various nuclei could be electrically stimulated. Using these techniques, researchers have managed to isolate two areas of the hypothalamus which seem of particular importance in the control of eating. They are the ventro-medial nucleus and the lateral hypothalamus. Ablations in the ventro-medial nucleus have been shown to result in what is known as hyperphagia (over-eating). The effect has been demonstrated successfully across a wide variety of species and in all cases the animals have become thoroughly obese (Mayer and Barnett, 1955). Researchers have also obtained the complementary finding that when the ventro-medial hypothalamus is electrically stimulated, eating is inhibited. It seems then that the cells in this nucleus operate rather like an off switch for hunger. In so far as this area of the hypothalamus, when active, seems to play an inhibitory role, it is reasonable to suppose that it might well be specifically inhibiting some other area which is involved in the control of hunger. Further research has located such an area to be the lateral hypothalamus.

Electrical stimulation of the lateral hypothalamus elicits eating behaviour. Small lesions in this area result in the animal refusing to eat (called *aphagia*). Such animals will in fact starve to death unless they are force-fed (Teitelbaum and Epstein, 1962). This result would seem to indicate that the lateral hypothalamus is responsible for the initiation of feeding. Such a view is further supported by another finding. When both areas (the ventro-medial and lateral) are ablated, the effect is the same as lesions to just the lateral area. In such cases the animals develop aphagia and starve.

The question of how the animal actually controls its eating in the normal state still remains outstanding. We seem to have discovered some sort of hunger centres, but what factors govern their operation? In so far as an animal stops eating long before any real nutritional effects occur, the switching off of eating behaviour must happen by virtue of some more immediate effects. This has led to a maintenance of interest in gastric and oral factors. Even though such peripheral mechanisms are not, as we have seen, absolutely necessary for long term regulation of eating, they have nevertheless been shown to have some more short term importance. For example, rats which have been given a solution of saccharine (a sweet but completely non-nutritive substance) subsequently show a slight decrease in the amount of food taken. Such an effect does not occur when the saccharine is delivered straight to the stomach. This finding clearly implicates oral factors as playing some part in the control of normal feeding. That gastric factors are also at work is demonstrated by the experiments which show that distension of the stomach leads to a subsequent reduction of food intake.

But it must be stressed again that animals without stomachs can still regulate their eating. What more primary sources of information could there be which could signal hunger-related events to the relevant centres in the hypothalamus? We now discuss some theories which have attempted to answer this question.

The glucostatic theory

The first theory, known as the glucostatic theory, is associated with Mayer (1955). This theory suggests that blood-sugar level may be a regulating factor in determining whether hunger is turned on or off. At first appearances, the level of sugar in the blood seems a promising regulating factor. However there existed, even at the time when Mayer first propounded his theory, an accumulation of evidence that was hardly favourable. It was well known, for example, that blood-sugar levels in humans who voluntarily underwent periods of fasting were likely to show very little variation over fairly long time intervals. When blood-sugar levels did vary, the variations did not in any way correlate with reported hunger pangs. Experiments have been done which have artificially induced changes in the blood-sugar level, but the results have been inconclusive. Hypoglaecemia (lowered blood-sugar level), as a result of injections of insulin, regularly produced eating activity. However the raising of blood-sugar levels (hyperglaecemia) did not have the clearly opposite effects which might be predicted. Obviously a simple blood-sugar theory seems unlikely.

Mayer was well aware of these difficulties and suggested that previous work had not taken the balance of blood-sugar into consideration. Previous experiments had estimated only absolute measures of blood-sugar in the system. Mayer put forward the idea that it was the amount of blood-sugar actually available for use that was really important. Such blood-sugar is to be found in the arteries not in the veins. In consequence he supposed that hunger existed only when the arterial supply fell so that there was little or no difference between the concentrations in the arterial and venous blood. This modified view of the importance of blood-sugar has received support. Certainly hypothalamic areas do seem to be sensitive to direct injections of glucose (Duner, 1953). Injections of glucagon (a hormone which raises blood-sugar level) have been shown to abolish speedily the experience of hunger and the occurrence of stomach contractions in human subjects (Stunkard *et al.*, 1955). Injections of ordinary glucose do not have this effect (Stunkard, 1957); this is especially favourable to Mayer's view since glucagon increases the difference between arterial and venous concentrations, whereas ordinary glucose does not. There are also a number of experiments which have shown that hyperglaecemia increases electrical activity in those areas of the brain associated with satiation, in particular the ventro-medial hypothalamus. Hypoglaecemia on the other hand has the opposite effect of decreasing such activity.

There have been some experiments which have obtained contradictory findings but they have tended to use rather insensitive measures of hunger. Mayer certainly does not claim that his theory provides a complete explanation of hunger motivation. He admits that, under normal conditions, many factors determine whether an animal eats or not. In human beings we know for a fact that we eat as much because of acquired habits or tastes as because of hunger. When a certain time of day comes round we get into the habit of eating at that time because it *is* lunch time or *is* dinner time. When we are invited out to dinner and the hostess serves a disastrous dessert, we eat it out of politeness even when hunger has taken flight at the first mouthful.

The thermal theory

Brobeck (1955) has sought to account for the regulation of eating by a thermal hypothesis. He proposes the existence of thermoreceptors (i.e. receptors sensitive to heat) in the hypothalamus which register changes of temperature. It is known that eating is followed by a slight rise in central body temperature and a somewhat larger rise in peripheral body temperature. Brobeck's view is that an animal eats in order to keep warm, and stops eating in order to avoid any excessive rise in central body temperature.

The experiment usually quoted as the major test of Brobeck's hypothesis was performed by Andersson and Larsson (1961). A cannula capable of circulating warm and cold water was implanted in the hypothalamus of a goat. The experimenters used the pre-optic and rostral areas known to be associated with temperature regulation. It was discovered that the cooling of the hypothalamus led to a commencement of eating. Warming, as was expected, caused a quick cessation of eating.

There are, however, criticisms of this experiment. Not least is the criticism that the range of temperatures used might well have been too wide to allow us to make any generalizations about thermal control under normal conditions. In addition, there have been a series of contradictory findings. Injections of amino acids, which should cause a rise in temperature, have not been shown to abolish or even decrease stomach contractions (Stunkard, 1957). Mayer and Greenberg (1953) found that hyperphagic rats in fact had higher body temperatures than normals, a result which seems somehow at odds with the thermal hypothesis. Although Brobeck's theory has been by no means totally refuted, it must be said that at present it does not have the same measure of support as the glucostatic theory. One thing is certain however: the existence of some sort of feedback mechanism is indisputable. The feedback might involve elements of Mayer's and Brobeck's theories, or other factors (e.g. levels of body fat – a lipostatic theory). The feedback in all events is likely to be complex and more than can be accounted for by just one factor.

Homeostasis

The term 'feedback' leads us to another important concept in motivation. That concept is *homeostasis*. The simplest and most easily comprehended example of a homeostatic mechanism is the familiar thermostat. This device, in keeping a constant temperature within a very small range, operates by continuously responding to feedback. When the temperature falls by only a small amount, this change is registered by the thermostat which then initiates the turning on of the heat supply. The temperature of course rises, and goes slightly above the setting. This information is in turn fed back to the thermostat which responds by turning off the heat supply. The thermostat is thus constantly monitoring changes in temperature within small limits and acting to reverse the situation when those limits are approached. Now it seems that the two centres in the hypothalamus which are associated with feeding play the crucial role in just such a homeostatic mechanism, each centre responding to important items of feedback.

It all seems rather neat and it is necessary to warn the

reader that the position is not really so settled. Those areas of the hypothalamus have indeed been shown to have importance in the regulation of eating, but it would be wrong to conclude that they are always involved in the response to feedback. For example animals will respond to lowered glucose availability even when the ventro-medial hypothalamus is ablated (Epstein, 1971). The idea of discrete on and off switches in particular areas of the hypothalamus is not too misleading as a first approximation. It is, however, an oversimplified picture, still being modified by current research.

Specific hunger

Richter (1942) removed the adrenal glands of rats. The adrenal glands have as one of their functions the regulation of salt uptake by the body. Richter supposed that the surgically prepared rats would make shifts in their diet in order to make up the salt loss which was now occurring. His hunch was found to be correct. Whereas preoperatively the rats had preferred a good deal more water solution to salt solution, after surgery they consistently chose the salt solution. Richter (1927) also showed that a rat, which was at liberty to choose its diet from a selection of all the foodstuffs essential to its survival, was able to match its intake very well to its physiological requirements. However animals are not always so naturally wise, and it goes without saying that humans are not. It is probably true that a natural ability to self-select one's diet does exist at root, but many factors including age and, most importantly, acquired habits interfere with and more often than not over-rule the body's so-called natural wisdom in this respect. For example, in one experiment rats which had already learned to show a preference for sugar solution rather than salt solution did not sufficiently abandon that preference even after removal of the adrenal glands. The result was that many of the experimental animals died of salt deficiency. Animals which had not learned the prior preference for sugar were found to adapt themselves well to the changed circumstances following surgery.

Richter has studied the phenomenon of specific hunger in some detail and has shown, for instance, how pregnancy causes a temporary change in dietary requirements. Pregnant rats are quite capable of self-selecting their food during pregnancy, and then returning to normal feeding after the litter has been weaned.

Although the phenomenon has been well documented, the nature of the mechanisms controlling self-selection of diet is by no means clear. Some of the explanations put forward are often no more than reformulations of the problem, e.g. that there are specific physiological needs which are aroused by specific deficits. However if this were the whole truth, why is it that self-selection often goes disastrously wrong? Some answer may be got from recent research which suggests that the key to this 'natural wisdom' might well be a gross predisposition on the part of any animal to respond with any change of diet when signs of deficiency become manifest. Such trial and error shifts would seem evolutionarily very sound. More than this we do not know.

Thirst

As in the case of hunger, the various theories about motivational mechanisms in thirst have split between peripheral and central ones. Indeed Cannon, the main protagonist of the peripheral theory of hunger, is also one of the early advocates of a peripheral theory of thirst. His idea was quite simply that thirst arises because of the experience of dryness in the mouth, which in turn is a direct consequence of the decreased output of the salivary glands. Of relevance to Cannon's theory were a whole number of experiments performed in the early part of this century with drugs which affected salivary flow. For example; atropine (a derivation of the notorious deadly nightshade) is known to reduce salivation and cause dryness of the mouth. Cannon observed that injections of this drug prompted drinking in his experimental subjects. However the findings with such drugs have not been conclusive, by any means. Montgomery (1931) administered atropine and a drug called pilocarpine, which has the opposite effect of stimulating salivation; the subjects were dogs. Some of the dogs had had their salivary glands surgically removed, whilst others had kept them intact. Little difference was reported in the amount of water imbibed by the different animals. Of course, great differences should have been found if the peripheral theory implicating dryness of mouth and salivary flow were correct. Bellows and VanWagenen (1939) threw doubt on the simple peripheral theory of thirst by showing that animals which had all the sensory nerves of the mouth region severed nevertheless continued to regulate their drinking satisfactorily. Also damaging to Cannon's theory are those observations which demonstrate the ability of subjects to discriminate and separate the experience of thirst and the experience of a dry mouth. Human subjects can certainly do this. Windsor (1930) showed that the chewing of gum caused a continuation of salivation in thirsty subjects; it did not however alter the subjects' sensations of thirst. Conversely it has been shown that men suffering from extreme thirst, perhaps after days in the desert, continue to drink and feel thirsty long after the sensation of a dry mouth has been assuaged. This would seem to indicate that so long as a water deficit remains to be made up, the subject still experiences thirst. Our conclusion must be that Cannon's theory is not adequately supported, and there certainly must be many more factors involved in the control of thirst than those envisaged in a peripheral 'dry mouth' theory.

One of these other factors which deserves mention is the role of the pituitary gland. It is known that the posterior pituitary is responsible for the releasing of a hormone called ADH (anti-diuretic hormone). This hormone released into the bloodstream, causes the kidneys to reabsorb water used in the production of urine. Verney (1947) advanced the theory that the critical controlling factor leading to the secretion of ADH by the pituitary is the osmotic pressure of the body fluids. Before we proceed further with Verney's theory and more recent developments we had better look at the meanings of some words which are essential to the argument. Those words are *osmotic pressure*, *isotonicity*, *hypotonicity*, and *hypertonicity*.

Suppose we have some sort of salt solution, where we can vary the concentration of the solute. Suppose also we have a membrane which is semi-permeable, i.e. admits some things to cross it and others not. Suppose now the semi-permeable membrane separates two solutions. If the two solutions are of equal concentration, the concentration of each remains unaltered and they are said to be isotonic. If, however, one solution is more concentrated it is said to be hypertonic and water will pass across the membrane and bring the two solutions into isotonicity. The less concentrated solution in this case is said to be hypotonic. The pressure resulting from these changes in tonicity is called osmotic pressure.

Now let us return to Verney's theory. He supposed that there were receptors in the carotid artery (the main blood supplier to the brain) which were sensitive to changes of osmotic pressure in the blood. When water is ingested in sufficient quantity, these receptors register the dilution of body fluid and transmit the information to the pituitary which then cuts down the supply of ADH. Consequently water, instead of being reabsorbed by the kidneys, is now excreted in urine. The osmotic pressure of the body fluids is thus increased. Receptors now register this change, and signal the pituitary to re-commence the secretion of ADH. In support of his theory, Verney showed that injections of hyptertonic saline directly into the carotid artery caused an immediate rise in the production of ADH by the pituitary.

We have not said so far anything about the mechanisms of thirst; we have simply pointed out that there does exist a means by which the brain can discover something about the state of tonicity of the body fluids. Since Verney's experiments other injections of hypertonic solutions have been shown to have similar effects to saline. Such solutions include glucose and sucrose. However, the idea that osmotic pressure is the sole factor is essentially incorrect. Fitzsimons (1971) shows that a substance called urea does not have the effect. This indicates something very important. The critical factor is not osmotic pressure *per se*, but is more likely to be cellular dehydration, which can of course result in increased osmotic pressure. The idea that thirst is associated just with increases of solute is ruled out on other grounds too. Cellular dehydration can result even when there is an excess of water, provided that the solute is more in excess than the water. The point is that any concentrated solution requires dilution and the body, in order to achieve this, has to give up water from the body cells. All the evidence points to the basic importance of cellular dehydration in the onset of thirst.

Verney was essentially concerned with the pituitary and its role in water regulation. Other experiments have shown that the motivational centre for thirst regulation is the hypothalamus itself. Andersson (1953) injected hypertonic saline into the hypothalamus of a goat, and elicited drinking behaviour in the presence of water. The importance of osmotic pressure was again confirmed by injections of hypotonic and isotonic solutions which failed to show the same effect. Injections of solution at other sites in the hypothalamus produced both drinking and ADH secretion from the posterior pituitary. Since Andersson's first result, these findings have been replicated in other species.

Thus the work on thirst has led very much in the same direction as the work on hunger. There does seem to exist a homeostatic mechanism in the hypothalamus which is responsive to signalled changes in the state of cellular hydration. However, before we complete our account of the central theory of thirst, we must mention two exceptions to the general parallel we have drawn with hunger.

First, it seems that there are two kinds of thirst. There is certainly the osmotic thirst which we have just described, arising from the hypertonicity of certain body fluids and the underlying dehydration of cells. However there exists research to show that thirst can also occur when there is no change in osmotic pressure of body fluids, but when there is lowered blood volume. Osmosis, though an important factor in thirst regulation, is certainly far from being the whole story.

The second difference between the research on hunger and that on thirst is that in the case of hunger we saw two reasonably separate centres in the hypothalamus: roughly speaking a hunger centre in the lateral hypothalamus and a satiety centre in the ventro-medial nucleus. In the research on thirst the search for a clear satiety centre goes on. It is true that a mechanism involving only one centre is possible and has indeed been suggested: we may merely state that the non-stimulation of the thirst centre switches off the behaviour of drinking. However, we should then have to explain why animals do stop drinking in a very precise and self-regulating way. They would over-drink considerably if they had to wait for cellular rehydration to be signalled to the hypothalamus via a change in osmotic pressure. Lastly, although more research has to be done, some experiments have shown that lesions in certain parts of the hypothalamus (particularly the lateral part) do abolish normal drinking.

The reason why we include sleep in a book on motivation is quite simply because in the adult person it takes care of almost a third of their lives and is motivational in the very obvious sense that we all patently express and manifest the need to sleep. Any need which requires so much time to be satisfied deserves some mention. And yet, for all this, no one can say at the present time what the function of sleep is. We know why we need to eat and drink. We know why, for the survival of a species, sexual activity is vital. No such *raison d'être* can be given for sleeping. Perhaps one might guess it has something to do with rest or recovery from fatigue, but this does not get us very far. Muscles can easily be relaxed without such a mammoth surrender of consciousness. If sleep has a function it has to be more complicated than that. We shall return to the speculations in this area when we have said something of what we do know about the pattern and process of sleep.

First, sleep is not synonymous with a loss of consciousness. On the contrary, the brain continues to be very active during periods of sleep, although the sleeper is relatively cut off from external stimuli. Even in this respect there are exceptions. A sleeper may not respond in any way to a loud noise such as the sound of a motor horn; he may well, however, register his own name being called urgently, even though the noise of the latter is considerably less. This suggests that to some extent stimuli are still being monitored by the sleeper and important messages are filtered through (see Oswald, 1966).

Another common view about sleep which has to be challenged is that it involves a lowering of activity. A video-recording of a person sleeping would show throughout the night periods of quite violent jerky movements. Concentration on the eyes would reveal periods of very rapid eye movements. In terms of actual neural activity within the brain it is extremely doubtful whether there is any overall decrease during sleep of the total number of neurones firing per second. Sleeping is not to be seen as a quiescent state, but as a different active state from waking.

Detailed investigation of the processes involved in sleep became possible with the introduction of the electroencephalograph (EEG), which gives an on-going record of

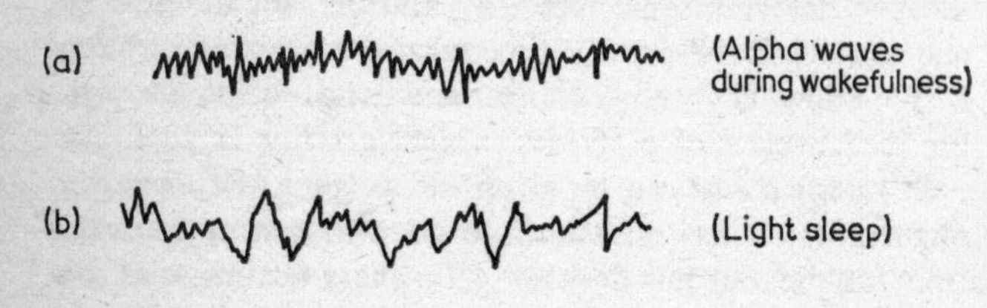

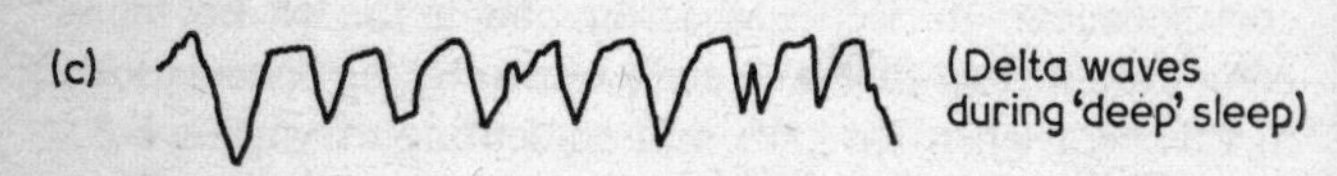

Fig. 3.1 *Brain-wave patterns during sleep and waking*

brain-waves. Researchers have built up a picture of the characteristic brain-waves which occur during sleeping and waking (see Fig. 3.1.) The typical EEG in the relaxed waking state shows low voltage, high frequency waves known as alpha waves. Drowsiness and light sleep lead to less alpha pattern and more waves of slower frequency, interrupted by brief bursts of very high frequency called spindles. During the first half of the night, this second stage is succeeded by waves of even slower frequency (delta waves) and the spindles become fewer. Finally stage four is reached where slow frequency waves completely dominate the picture and spindles may be virtually absent. The exact labelling of the stages can be a difficult job and workers in this area have recourse to a published list of criteria for scoring their records. In addition to the stages mentioned above, researchers have also found an extraordinary EEG, almost identical to the waking picture, which occurs periodically during sleep and comes in fact to dominate the picture during the final period. These particular EEGs correlate well with the rapid eye movements (REMs) which we mentioned earlier. These periods of REM sleep are also associated with reports of dreaming. One is more likely to elicit dream reports if one wakes a subject during REM sleep than during non-REM sleep. That is not to say, however, that dreaming is solely a function of REM periods, but dream reports during the non-REM period seem to be vaguer.

What is the major controlling factor in sleep? Deep in the subcortical structures of the brain, extending from the medulla of the lower brain stem to the thalamus, there is a dense network of neurons which is known as the *reticular activating system* (RAS). This area has been implicated in the control of sleeping and waking (see Moruzzi, 1964). High frequency electrical stimulation of the ascending RAS induces both EEG arousal and behavioural awakening in a sleeping animal. If, on the other hand, the brain stem higher up is sectioned, then the result is a synchronized EEG and a behaviourally comatose animal. This waking centre in the brain is known, after its discoverers, as the 'ascending reticular activating system of Moruzzi and Magoun'. The search for sleep centres came later, and the reason it did come later was that the early theories of sleep tended to think of the state of sleep being due to a passive deactivation of the waking system. There seemed evidence for this view from the common observation that we normally prepare for sleep by cutting out as much information from the senses as possible: we turn off the light and close our eyes; we make sure we are neither too hot nor too cold; in exceptionally noisy circumstances we may put in ear-plugs.

Later theorists came to believe that there were active sleep centres which actually counteracted the waking system. Much work was done to find these centres by electrode implantation and stimulation. Centres mushroomed all too quickly in the literature, possibly because the main experimental animal used was the cat, who spends so much time asleep anyway that it makes it very easy to think one has discovered a sleep centre. The merit of the work, however, is in its clear acceptance that sleep, like waking, must involve active systems in the brain. The most important experiments of recent years have been those which have shown that damage to certain parts of the brain can result in an animal which is constantly awake. Much of this work has been done by the French scientist Michel Jouvet.

In the same general subcortical region we have mentioned already (between medulla and thalamus) there exist along the midline of the brain-stem what are called the raphe nuclei. Complete destruction of these leads to an almost permanent wakefulness. If the area is only partially damaged then there is a good correlation between the amount of damage and the degree of resulting sleep loss. Not only does this area seem to be a general sleep centre, but there are clues also to the biochemistry of sleep. The neurons of the region contain serotonin (one of the brain's chemical transmitter substances). Destruction of the raphe nuclei leads to a decrease in the quantity of cerebral serotonin. The quantity of the other major chemical transmitter, noradrenalin, remains unaltered. The results would appear to show that the cerebral monoamines, including serotonin, are of some importance to the mechanisms involved in sleep.

Once again in the brain-stem, at the level of the pons, is an area called the locus coerulus. This area has been isolated by Jouvet (1967) as being the centre controlling REM sleep. When it is lesioned, REM sleep is suppressed. The neurons in this region are rich in noradrenalin, and it would seem that it plays a parallel role in REM sleep to that of serotonin in slow-wave sleep.

Now let us return to the function of sleep. REM sleep is the easiest to speculate about since it, at least, is not found equally in all species. As a general rule REM sleep becomes more frequent the higher one moves up the evolutionary scale. Reptiles exhibit none; birds show only short bursts; mammals a lot more. If one looks at the individual species there is a strong trend which indicates that 'hunters' (typically the cat family) show enormous periods of REM sleep, whereas 'hunted' species, such as rabbits, show very little. But REM sleep is not just a luxury born out of a usually unthreatened night's sleep. It can be shown that we exhibit a need to have REM sleep. If an animal is deprived selectively of such sleep, it will make up the deficit later by devoting a much larger part of its total sleep to REM activity. This selective 'rebound' after deprivation also occurs with other sleep stages too. One interpretation of this data is that certain chemical substances accumulate in the nervous system during deprivation. The elimination of chemical substances in the nervous system is one function which has been suggested for sleep. But what about the experience of dreaming? Do dreams have a purpose? All is speculation. Perhaps, comparing the brain with a computer, tapes have to be cleared, altered, or erased. Jouvet has suggested that dreaming is the replaying and updating of our genetic codes. Finally, Jouvet may be permitted the last word: 'sleep remains one of the great mysteries of neurophysiology'.

Sex

It is common for people to classify hunger, thirst and sex together as basic animal drives. The discussion which follows should convince one that this is somewhat inaccurate. It might make sense to talk of hunger and thirst as *drives*, since in a way the animal is driven to activity by certain bodily depletions; in other words the animal works to make up a deficit. This is hardly true in the case of sexual activity. Rather, sex is an appetite, and the role of external factors in controlling (or failing to control) that appetite becomes paramount, the higher one moves up the evolutionary scale.

However, there are physiological factors which must be considered. First, the sexual organs themselves can be considered a source of stimulation. It has been suggested that sensations of tension in the penis of the male, or the vagina of the female, form the basis of sexual activity. But the absolute necessity of such peripheral factors is disputed on the evidence from many sources that gross surgical interference does not put an end to sexual activity. Another major physiological factor in sexual activity is the role of sex hormones. The degree to which hormones control sexual behaviour varies from species to species, but we can begin with a few general observations. The anterior pituitary gland releases hormones called *gonadotrophins*, which in turn stimulate the gonads (testes in the male, ovaries in the female), to produce their own hormones. In general, the male produces the hormone *testosterone*, and the female produces *oestrogen* and *progesterone*. The importance of these hormones, particularly in animals lower down the scale than man, cannot be overemphasized. It is known that the reflexes necessary for sexual behaviour are present long before puberty. Orgasm (obviously without ejaculation) can be seen in the human male infant (Kinsey, Pomeroy and Martin, 1948). The injection of pituitary or gonadal hormones can be demonstrated to produce sexual behaviour in a number of pre-pubertal animals. Research with rats has shown that animals castrated in infancy nevertheless will later show complete copulatory behaviour, following hormone injections. Removal of the pituitary, on the other hand, does lead to impaired sexual development.

In the case of females, the factors controlling sexual

activity may, in the simplest cases, merely be seasonal. In higher species, regular 'heat' (oestrus) periods determine sexual receptivity, and these 'heat' periods are under hormonal control. In the highest primates, including man, the importance of hormonal control becomes much less pervasive, whilst environmental factors gain almost complete ascendancy. The administration of hormones to human subjects does not normally have clear-cut effects. The overriding importance of learning and conditioning means, for example, that injections of testosterone are not necessarily going to cure impotence (Ford and Beach, 1951). The results for humans are not paralleled in the case of lower animals. Here, injections of appropriate hormones do indeed have a direct effect on sexual activity. Moreover, it has been possible to show that both sexes have the capacity for both male and female behaviour, depending on the balance of hormones achieved.

As well as hormonal control of sexual activity, we need to mention the control exercised by the nervous system itself. Certain reflexes are governed by just the spinal cord. However, when we start talking about the integration of these reflexes in an orderly mating sequence, we have to move to the brain itself. We have already mentioned in our discussion of thirst, the intimate connection between the hypothalamus and the pituitary, so it is not surprising to find that damage to parts of the hypothalamus can impair sexual activity through its effect on the pituitary. Far more important from our point of view is the role of the cerebral cortex, i.e. the most highly developed part of the brain. Removal of about half this area eliminates sexual activity in males of the higher species completely. There is reason to believe, however, that female sexual activity, though impaired, is not so affected. The conclusion is that male sexual activity in higher animals depends critically on the arousal functioning of the cerebral cortex. This increasing cortical control parallels the observation that experience and social learning also become crucial factors in higher primates and man. In such cases, if one destroys the cortex, no amount of male hormone injections will reinstate sexual activity.

We are already beginning to see that sexual activity in man depends more on external than internal stimulation, and this brings us back to the point we made earlier about sex being an appetite rather than a drive. Deprivation studies have reinforced this view, even in the case of the rat. A standard way of gauging motivational strength is to put an electrified barrier between an animal and its goal. Using this technique, researchers have recorded how many times a rat will cross the barrier in order to copulate with a partner. It has been shown that the number of crossings does not increase over a period varying from one to twenty-five days of sexual abstinence in the male rat. There is indeed a *refractory* period after orgasm for all male animals, but after this, sexual activity is not related to deprivation, except that prolonged copulatory sessions do lead to progressively longer refractory periods. Even after repeated copulation to the point of exhaustion, it has been shown in one study (Beach and Jordan, 1956) that over 70 per cent of male rats are back to normal in three days. In female mammals (except women, of course) the oestrus cycle determines sexual activity. But even here, during the period of 'heat', copulation does not act as a decreaser of motivation, once again casting doubt on the use of the word 'drive' in this context. In the case of women, it has been reported that sexual desire does tend to peak, either immediately before or after menstruation. However this has not been found universally in all cultures and it would seem that apparent relationships between physiology and sexual desire may be more apparent than real. In conclusion, we may restate the view that sex is not a drive which surges up as a function of deprivation. The emphasis when hormonal control is minimal must be on sources of external stimulation, to which we now turn. However, the comparison between sex as an appetite and hunger and thirst as drives, may be a little overdone. We have seen that eating behaviour, for example, is not just a function of hours of food deprivation, but can depend on externally derived habits.

There are, of course, very general environmental determinants of sexual activities, such as time of day. Diurnal animals tend to copulate in the daytime, nocturnal animals at night. Man is the exception, preferring to copulate at night, without being a nocturnal animal, but this probably only began after Eve ate a certain apple. The desire for excessive privacy, even from one's partner, is peculiarly human. Familiarity with the setting seems to be important in other animals as well as man. Strangeness of surroundings tends to disrupt performance. For some animals there are other general features of the environment – temperature, presence of water, rocks, plants etc., which prepare the path of love-making, but human beings do not tend to be so fetishistic, unless one includes a propensity for a double bed.

If we move on to specific stimuli provided by the partner, differences between species are innumerable in both the nature of stimulation (visual, tactile, chemical etc.) and in the exact role of such stimulation. A stimulus may just have an arousing property and its absence would not be crucial; alternatively, it may be an absolute and necessary condition of the mating continuing. Ritual behaviours elicited by specific stimuli in the service of a mating instinct have been dealt with elsewhere (see Ch. 2) and tend to be confined to lower animals. In the higher animals, external stimuli tend only to play an arousing role.

The stimulating practices of the human species vary enormously from culture to culture. Even with a culture they vary considerably from one group to another. Kinsey and his co-workers (1948, 1953) have documented such practices as they exist and vary in the United States. If the reader wishes to trace the tortuous path of American love-making from the missionary simplicity of the lower socio-economic classes, to the dizzy heights of oral love amongst the higher classes, then he is referred to Kinsey's work. He ought, however, to bear in mind that his information may be out of date, though not, the present writer suspects, by very much.

To proceed any further with a discussion of the external stimuli affecting humans would not be very fruitful, precisely because of the almost infinite variety which results from different experiences and conditioning.

Summary

1 *Hunger*. Factors controlling the regulation of eating cannot be peripheral – animals can still, for example, control their food intake satisfactorily after gastrectomy. Central theories have pointed to the importance of hypothalamic centres and a homeostatic regulation of food intake by means of feedback. Such feedback probably includes information about sugar availability in the blood. Other factors are probably involved also. The phenomenon of specific hunger has been demonstrated, but the mechanisms underlying it are still obscure.

2 *Thirst*. Peripheral theories of thirst, such as the 'dry mouth' theory have been discredited. Central theories stress the importance of feedback concerning the state of cellular dehydration which follows water deficits. Centres in the hypothalamus which respond to such feedback are being investigated. There are two kinds of thirst: osmotic and volemic. Osmotic thirst results from the hypertonicity of body fluids. Volemic thirst results from overall lowered blood volume.

3 *Sleep*. The function of sleep is not known. Stages of

sleep can be identified using an EEG. Most sleep involves slow waves, but there exists a sleeping desynchronized EEG, which correlates with rapid eye movements and dream reports. Sleep is an active state, rather than just a passive absence of the waking state. There seem to be centres in the brain which control sleeping and waking. REM sleep seems to have its own centre. Biochemical factors have been implicated. The function of sleep is the one great mystery for neurophysiology.

4 *Sex.* Sex is more an appetite than a drive. External stimuli in the higher animals play a much more important part than internal factors. Hormonal control is important in lower animals.

4
Drive theory

The biological bases of motivation which we have discussed so far are to be seen as setting limits on our behaviour. When all is said and done, we are forced to spend a certain amount of our time eating, drinking, and sleeping. We now move on to an analysis of behaviour in a wider sense, taking in those behaviours which are acquired through the interaction of an organism with its environment.

At the very beginning of the book we gave a picture of a rat running through a maze of activities. We might just as well look at human behaviour from any street corner, where we would see a multitude of people scurrying in all directions, making, as the saying goes, their separate ways. What role does motivation play in determining learned behaviour? We could point to the goals and objectives which organisms seek, and point to these as explanations of behaviour. But is this any more than commonsense. Question: why did you go out? Answer: to buy a bottle of wine. Why are you lying down? Because I'm tired. The reasons we give for behaving in every day life help us to *understand* behaviour, they do not *explain* it. In many cases we look to the future in order to give a common-sense type 'explanation', since the goal lies at the end of a sequence of responses. As well as this automatically giving the attributes of cognition and foresight to the agent, it suggests that such cognition and foresight somehow has a hand in the determination of the behaviour. We might admit this for our human subjects but what about monkeys? Shall we give them cognition so automatically? And if we do, shall we extend it to the laboratory rat?

One of the most fundamental canons of psychological explanation was given by Lloyd Morgan in the late nineteenth century when he said that on no account should an animal's behaviour be explained by reference to a higher psychological process if it can be attributed to a lower one. We should bear this in mind even when we are considering explanations of human behaviour. Psychologists with a total commitment to Lloyd Morgan's canon were responsible for the development of an extremely mechanistic conception of how the behaviour of organisms is acquired and maintained (see F1). Of primary importance in their mechanistic conception has been the concept of *drive*. In their view, the behaviour of all organisms should, initially at least, be approached from the same standpoint as the behaviour of inanimate objects, i.e. by examining the force that pushes an entity into action. Such theorists have wanted to avoid a discussion about the purposes their organisms might or might not have. The reason is quite simple. Their search is for a psychological science which predicts the behaviour of organisms as objectively and as mechanistically as a physicist deals with atoms. Even when human beings are credited with consciousness of purpose and intention, the true mechanistic psychologist is apt to think of this as an epiphenomenon, i.e. something that exists but is aside from and irrelevant to the determination of behaviour. Behaviour is resolutely determined by historical factors in the organism's history, not by such teleological considerations as knowledge of future consequences. What is the nature of this force, this drive, which mechanically and blindly goads and determines our actions? To answer that question we must look to the work of one particular psychologist who has had by far the greatest influence on the study of motivation within psychology. His name is Clark Hull, and it is true to say that he dominated the psychology of learning and motivation throughout the 'thirties and 'forties, and the system he created for the analysis of behaviour remains very influential even today.

This is not a book about learning, so it would not be appropriate to describe Hull's mammoth edifice of learning theory in any more detail than is required to look at his theory of motivation (see A3). Basically Hull believed that learning was about the formation of habits or bonds between stimuli and responses. These S-R connexions explained the direction of all acquired behaviour. They were cemented by the operation of reinforcement, which is a term roughly synonymous with reward. But the animal will not embark on the execution of its conditioned responses unless some force pushes it into action. Hull used the word 'drive' to describe this force. He also laid down in the postulates of his system what he considered the sources of drive to be. All drive, in his view, was traceable to primary tissue needs: the need for food and water, the need for air, correct temperature, the need to get rid of waste products by micturition and defecation, the need for rest and sleep, and the need to avoid damage to tissue. These needs were postulated as the source of internal drive stimuli which had two important functions. First, they energized behaviour. They provided the 'push' which sent an organism into a learning situation. Secondly, the drive stimuli were thought to be the key to the all important process of reinforcement. Habits were strengthened if they succeeded in diminishing the intensity of drive. Drive reduction, then, was the nature of reinforcement.

Of course real life behaviour, even for an animal as

simple as the laboratory rat, is not usually an isolated response, but more often a rather long sequence of responses leading to some preferred goal, where presumably some reinforcement occurs. How does Hull explain this more complicated learning? First, Hull postulates that immediate reinforcement is more effective in forming habits than delayed reinforcement. Thus when a rat is put in a complex maze and makes its way towards a goal box, Hull expects that those errors made near the goal box will be corrected and the right responses learned before those errors more distant from the goal box. The reason for this prediction is, of course, that the correct responses near the goal box are more immediately followed by reinforcement. But for long sequences of behaviour, where delay of reinforcement may be considerable, Hull allows for bridging reinforcement. Reinforcement itself can be acquired. *Primary* reinforcement may be drive reduction, but we do not always behave as if this were the goal. Certain outcomes can become reinforcing in their own right, if these outcomes have been encountered regularly in close contiguity with primary reinforcement.

A simple demonstration of this acquired (or secondary) reinforcement can be seen in an experiment by Bugelski (1938). If rats are trained to press a bar in order to receive a reward of food, it is possible to get the animal to stop performing this response (we say *extinguish* the response) by failing to give a food reward. Let us now suppose that some animals as well as having received food have been receiving also a click sound from the apparatus whenever the bar is pressed. A click is not a primary reinforcer in so far as it does not satisfy any primary source of drive. However, if those rats which have been receiving the click continue to receive it throughout the extinction period (i.e. the period when food is withheld) then they will have a much greater resistance to extinction – they go on pressing the bar for a much longer period – in the absence of primary reinforcement. This is the result which Bugelski got, and one interpretation of it is that the click by association with the food in the learning situation becomes a secondary reinforcer.

We can see that secondary reinforcement is a valuable part of the Hullian framework allowing for the greater application of his theory outside simple maze learning situations. However it does not help to answer the motivational question of what pushes us into activity when primary drive does not seem to be apparent. Certainly secondary reinforcement can explain a long sequence of behaviour when the delay of primary reinforcement may seem enormous, but the motivational push still comes from the primary drive source. Also when the chain to primary reinforcement is broken, the secondary reinforcement eventually loses all its efficacy in maintaining the acquired behaviour. Thus the rats in Bugelski's experiment did not carry on pressing the bar just for the click *ad infinitum*. Click without food maintained the behaviour of pressing the bar significantly, but only for a limited period. Similarly Cowles (1937) has shown that monkeys will work for poker chips if these can later be exchanged for primary food reinforcement. But, once again, when the chain to primary reinforcement is broken and the food is not forthcoming, the poker chips very soon lose all their secondary reinforcing properties. If we wish to explain behaviour, particularly human behaviour, which does not have primary need satisfaction as its instigator, and if we want to keep Hull's basic view that all motivation is ultimately grounded in the organism's biological needs as expressed through primary drive, then we must seek to establish the existence not so much of secondary reinforcers but *secondary drive*. As Hull says, speaking on this very question, given that 'motivation is an energizing process having its roots in organismic physiology, how do dollar bills, praise of others, and the word "good" come to energize and reinforce behaviour?' How do we acquire the drive to work for these very obviously effective reinforcers?

Fear as acquired drive

The literature on acquired drive has fixed itself very firmly on one what we might call 'master' acquired drive, and that is fear. The archetypal experiment demonstrating fear as an acquired drive was performed by Neal Miller in 1948. Rats were put in a two-compartment box, one part painted black, the other white. They were consistently shocked only in the white compartment. Before long the rats had very little time for the white compartment and retreated quickly to the safety of the black. We should like to say that the white box had itself come to evoke fear. Or perhaps more accurately we should say that the internal responses of the animal to the shock were now being elicited by the white box cues. Miller supposed that these conditioned stimuli were aversive to the animal, much in the same way as internal stimuli associated with food deprivation, and that they would have the properties of drive stimuli. Miller demonstrated such motivational properties by getting his experimental animals to learn a new response (turning a wheel), in order to escape from the white box. This finding seemed to show very clearly that 'fear' as a drive could be learned. It also caused a change in basic drive theory. Instead of needs being necessarily the roots of drive, the main property of drive was thought to accrue from the aversive intensity of internal stimulation. Reinforcement was the reduction of intense internal stimuli. Frustration of needs became simply a very obvious method of creating the necessary stimulation.

The initial experiment by Miller gave the impetus during the 'fifties for a lot of work on the nature of avoidance learning. The issue had always been a bit of a sore thumb because the learning of avoidance responses had never appeared to fit into the paradigm of Hull's learning theory. Let us look at the general phenomenon. When an animal is given warning of shock it can usually anticipate events and avoid the shock altogether by making the appropriate avoidance response before the onset of shock. This behaviour, once it is learned, is extremely resistant to extinction. One can remove the source of shock and the animal may well go on responding to the feared warning stimulus *ad infinitum*. This suggests that the avoidance behaviour comes to have its own reinforcement built in. But what is the nature of this reinforcement? It cannot be the cessation of shock, because as we have seen, once the learning is accomplished the shock becomes redundant. The problem is solved by invoking fear as a source of acquired drive in the situation. Miller and Mowrer, the key researchers in this area, both developed theories along these lines. According to Mowrer's two factor theory, 'fear' responses are classically conditioned (see A3) to the shock situation, in particular to any warning stimulus which immediately and reliably precedes the delivery of shock. These fear responses are a source of powerful internal drive stimuli for the animal. It is thus driven into activity, makes a successful avoidance response, and is reinforced by the diminution of those same internal fear stimuli. Once the important step of seeing fear both as a response conditionable to external stimuli, and as a drive capable of energizing and reinforcing avoidance responding is taken, this form of learning presents no particular problem for learning theory. The skeptical reader may well feel that the delegation of key processess in this form of learning to an unobservable internal mediation is suspect (see Dunham, 1971). However the conceptual analysis has clearly been of paramount use to the avowed drive theorist, as we shall see.

Fear, then, seems easily acquired as a drive. It is a more complicated business to condition a new drive by pairing it with an appetitively related drive source such as hunger or thirst. The 'drive' in the type of experiment we have just considered is easily controlled in terms of the onset and offset of electric shock. This is not the case with hunger and thirst. Here the task of pairing something precisely with the conditions of drive onset is an extremely difficult problem to solve. Indeed, the literature is divided on the question of whether it is possible to condition drives at all in this way. It is no surprise therefore that fear, as acquired drive, has become the major explanatory weapon in the hands of those who have wished to maintain a mechanistic drive theory in the analysis of behaviour.

For example J. S. Brown (1953) has suggested that the complexities of human motivation, though they may seem far removed from primary biological needs, are no longer beyond the explanatory grip of drive theory once fear is allowed to mediate behaviour. Why do we spend so much time in our life in search of such reinforcers as money and performing various operant responses (such as holding down a job) in order to receive the blessings of this particular reinforcer? (see A3) As a first answer we may invoke secondary reinforcement as a principle. Money, like the tokens earned by the monkeys in Cowle's experiment, bridges the gap to primary reinforcement. But this seems a bit far-fetched. One doubts whether many human products of Western civilization have ever had the kind of learning experiences which would lead to money becoming such a direct secondary reinforcer. More telling as an objection to the secondary reinforcement suggestion is the fact that money-seeking behaviour tends to develop an impetus of its own, and any chain back to primary reinforcement is redundant. A millionaire gleefully packing in his second million must be keeping a very shadowy wolf away from the door. It seems then that the primary drives, however devious their operation, cannot provide the motivational basis for such behaviour.

Brown suggests that instead we should turn these sorts of example on their heads and ask not what the person is seeking, but what the person is avoiding. A person can be said to be making money, or afraid of not making money. What we have to postulate here as a learning experience is not, on the face of it, unlikely. People live in a society where money (or more precisely the lack of it) is talked about with worried looks and lined faces. These faces become linked to the subject of money. It is learned that money reduces conditioned anxiety. The responses and sequences of behaviour that go into pursuing it are reinforced by diminishing the fear that motivates and energizes the behaviour. This manner of argument can obviously generate plausible accounts of most human appetitive behaviour, where the operation of primary drive seems most implausible.

The nature of drive

It is natural when talking about hunger, thirst, etc. to call these *drives*, in the plural. But we must try and resist the temptation. Hull was very careful to insist on the singular form, drive. Although drive could have different sources, the energizing force was thought of as one conglomerate, blindly energizing whatever habits an organism had acquired. Thus drive sources could combine, and Hull in these cases talks of the *pooled drive*. All sources of drive are pooled to determine the drive level of the organism. This then interacts multiplicatively with the strength of the relevant habit to determine a measure of how the animal actually will perform. Thus

$$P = H \times D$$

where P is performance potential; H is habit strength; and D is drive level.

Experiments have been done to illustrate the non-specificity of drive. Thus Kendler (1945) showed that animals trained to press a bar for food resisted extinction processes if they were under the condition of a new drive source, such as thirst. Meryman (1952) found that avoidance responses were facilitated when food deprivation added to the drive already created by acquired fear. Gray and Smith (1969) have shown the same sort of thing in reverse. Mild amounts of drive resulting from aversive experience can actually invigorate an appetitive response such as eating. Only in higher degrees will aversively derived drive energize new avoidance habits.

Conflict

Life is very much about making decisions. In so far as a decision suggests more than one alternative for action, and in so far as each alternative probably has its pros and cons, decision is tantamount to conflict. What behavioural principles governing conflict can be derived from drive theory?

Conflict can be defined as being motivated to respond in more than one way, when the responses are incompatible. A child may be offered the choice between two kinds of icecream and find the choice very difficult. Psychologists talk of this as an approach-approach conflict. It is fairly easily resolved because once the choice is made, perhaps eventually through chance factors such as one icecream being nearer than the other, the conflict vanishes. The satisfying effect of the chosen icecream causes the attraction of the recently dismissed competitor to pall. Another source of conflict is known as avoidance-avoidance conflict. This can be neatly summed up as being between the devil and the deep blue sea. But once again such conflicts tend to be fairly easily, if resignedly, resolved, perhaps by a statement such as 'better the devil one knows than the devil one does not'. The most enduring and neurotic of conflicts involves approach and avoidance. In an approach-avoidance conflict random moves away from the courses of action do not help. The person cannot say to himself 'well, I've decided' because the very thing he wants to approach he also wants to avoid. The result is neurotic indecision. Governments faced with the choices of unemployment or inflation feel themselves to be in just such a conflict: benefits necessarily entail trouble.

Neal Miller made it his task to try and predict the behaviour of organisms in this kind of conflict situation simply by using the principles of Hullian theory. Performance as we have just seen is a function of drive level and habit strength. When an organism approaches the goal the performance improves. The tendency to approach is invigorated. If the animal is motivated by hunger, presumably the drive level is little altered between the start box and the goal box. The invigorated approach tendency nearer the goal box is mainly the result of the habit strength of those nearer responses being greater (remember the postulate concerning the immediacy of reinforcement). But what of the avoidance tendency? If this is a function of fear, then we are no longer dealing with a relatively static motive such as hunger. Here, the drive level increases as the organism approaches the feared situation, and will peak when the feared goal is reached. Thus if we were to plot gradients of approach and avoidance by looking at the strength of these separate tendencies at varying distances from the conflict-ridden goal box, we should expect the approach tendency to be higher than the avoidance tendency at areas distant from the goal (where hunger is high, but fear is hardly yet aroused at all). As the goal box approaches we should expect that the cues will elicit increasingly more fear, whilst hunger is not significantly increased. Thus the fear avoidance gradient will increase and overtake the less steeply rising approach gradient. This is illustrated in Figure 4.1.

It can be see that when the organism reaches the point where the lines intersect, and where the approach and avoidance tendencies are therefore equal, we should expect true conflict behaviour. If the animal moves forward it will

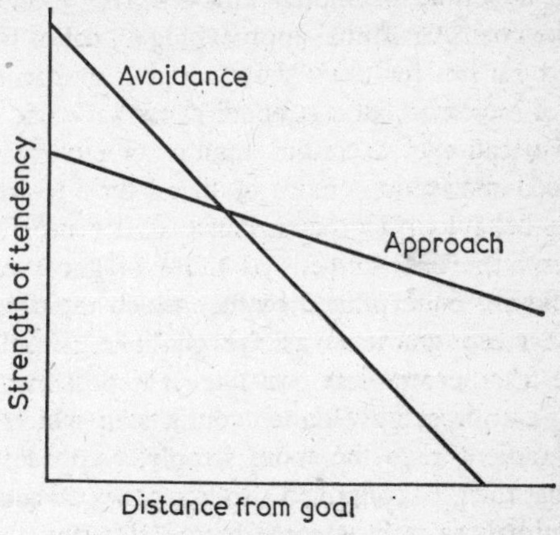

Fig. 4.1

experience actionable fear; if, on the other hand, it moves back it will so diminish its fear that it will be motivated to step forward again. Everything then conspires to keep the poor creature at the agony point of the intersection.

All so far has been hypothetical and predicted solely by the application of Hullian theory. Miller and his co-researchers went on to investigate whether his predictions stood the test of experimentation. Rats were equipped with little harnesses which were attached to apparatus which could measure how strongly the animals were pulling. This was done for those conditions in which the animal was pulling away from the goal, and for those conditions in which the animal was approaching it. Gradients of approach and avoidance could thus be obtained. The predictions of drive theory were confirmed. The approach gradients were not as steep as the avoidance gradients.

Now it would be wrong to conclude from what has been said that avoidance gradients are *always* steeper than approach gradients. The true import of the argument is that the gradient most dependent on environmental stimulation as a source of motivation will rise more steeply nearer the goal. An animal approaching a goal of food, and motivated by hunger does show a rising gradient, partly because of increased habit strength as we have said already, and also because of a certain amount of environmentally conditioned motivation (more of that later). However the approach behaviour in this instance is not nearly so dependent on the environment as the avoidance responses, since these are underpinned by fear which rapidly falls off (giving a steep gradient) as the goal-like stimuli which elicit the fear become less goal-like. It is possible, though, to imagine approach-avoidance conflicts in which the approach gradient rises the more steeply. Suppose, for example, that the goal contained a source of sexual satisfaction for an animal, as well as some feared situation. Now, we saw in the previous chapter that sexual motivation is much related to external arousing factors. We might suppose therefore in this case that the approach gradient would (if the sexual goal was attractive enough) rise very steeply and the situation for approach-avoidance conflict pictured in Figure 4.1. would be reversed.

Drive theory and human experimentation

We have seen that drive theorists put a lot of emphasis on fear and anxiety in the motivation of much human behaviour. A certain amount of research has been done to test theoretically derived hypotheses in the field of human verbal learning and the effects of anxiety.

Drive interacts with habit strength to create a performance variable, called by Hull reaction potential. But incorrect responses as well as correct responses have some potential for action. Drive, as we have seen, is a non-specific force and energizes incorrect as well as correct responses. Add to this a postulate that different responses have different thresholds for their elicitation and we have enough theory to make some predictions about actual behaviour.

One prediction is as follows. Subjects, high in anxiety, should be better than subjects low in anxiety at simple verbal learning tasks. In more complex tasks the reverse should be the case. The reason for these predictions is that increased drive will have a clearly superior effect when it energizes behaviour where the correct response is well-established or easily learned, and where the chances of energizing competing incorrect responses is less. That is the situation when we consider easy tasks. In more difficult tasks the prediction changes. Increased drive will only help to bring above threshold those already quite pre-potent responses which compete with the one correct response.

These predictions were tested by two of Hull's disciples, Kenneth Spence and Janet Taylor. Their learning tasks involved the use of paired-associates (see A6). Two words are given, one after the other, and the subject has to learn to reply to the first word of the pair with the second. Paired associates allow for differentiation of easy and difficult levels of association – an easy association would be something like 'boy-girl' or 'table-chair'. Spence and Taylor also investigated two kinds of subject: those high in anxiety and those low. Taylor devised a special scale for measuring anxiety level which is called the 'Taylor Manifest Anxiety Scale'. It was found by these researchers that high anxiety subjects did better with the easy word associations, but fared worse with the difficult list. Here then we see the mechanistic notions of drive theory meeting with some success when applied not to rats in mazes but to rather complicated human learning. Whether or not drive theory is the only or indeed the best explanation of the results is a different matter.

We have now completed a look at the main characteristics of the theory and seen some of its coverage. It is now time to see drive theory under attack.

The importance of incentives

The mechanistic approach to behaviour is to view performance of a response as being determined solely by habit and drive. Habits are the forged out motorways between starting-point (stimulus) and destination (response); drive is the fuel which makes the journey possible. However, given a certain starting point and a ready supply of fuel the destination, in this analogy, can never be in question, and certainly 'knowledge' of destination is irrelevant to the inexorability of the journey. Thus incentives can only enter our so far simple model of motivated behaviour as something of an embarrassment. Incentives suggest an effect on performance and yet the very thing one wishes to deny is that something in the future such as an incentive can have any effect on behaviour prior to it in time. Such a view, it would appear, goes completely counter to the principles of historical causation, which to some is the hallmark of scientific explanation.

It is therefore no accident that the study of incentives was fostered early on not by the Hullians but by those early cognitivists who were ready to admit 'expectations' into their psychological framework. The most notable of those antagonistic to Hull's stimulus-response psychology was Tolman, and an early experiment by Tolman and Honzig (1930) proved important in that it required serious modification of Hull's theory. The experiment is known as the 'latent learning experiment'.

Three groups of rats were introduced into a maze-solving situation. One group received a reward in the goal box on every trial. The second group never received a reward. The third group had the food reward introduced on the eleventh trial. What Tolman and Honzig showed was that the initial superiority of group I over group III was eroded suddenly and dramatically as soon as food was introduced (see Fig. 4.2). Now this could hardly be due to

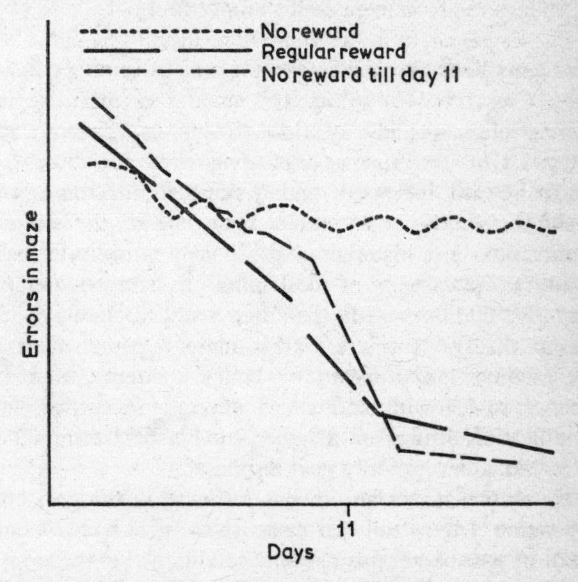

Fig. 4.2 *After Tolman and Honzig, 1930*

a change in habit strength, since Hull conceives of habit building up slowly in an incremental fashion as a result of reinforcement. The sudden change in performance must therefore be due to a change in the motivation of the animals. Since drive is constant for all the animals, the change in motivation must be dependent on incentive factors. Notice too that this experiment proves embarrassing for Hull's theory in another way. According to Hull, there can be no learning without reinforcement (drive reduction); habit strength is actually calculated on the basis of the number of reinforced trials. And yet the rats in group III which suddenly prove themselves so proficient in the task after trial eleven have, up till then, received no obvious reinforcement. To circumnavigate that difficulty, Hullians would have to postulate the prior existence of secondary reinforcement in the empty goal box.

But let us return to the question of incentives. Other experiments have also shown the effect of these on performance. Crespi (1942) shifted the amount of incentive for groups of rats mid-way through his experiment, and showed that performance was invigorated for those rats whose reward increased, and diminished for those who changed to a lesser incentive. Now one of the striking observations any historian of psychology is likely to make concerns the capacity of the Hullians to accept seemingly cognitive findings and fit them into a still resolutely mechanistic theory. Nowhere is this more apparent than in the modification proposed by Hull's colleague, Kenneth Spence, to deal with motivational effects of incentives. The modification centres on a rather cumbersome term called a 'fractional anticipatory goal response'.

An animal makes an obvious response in the goal box, say eating. Let us call that response the goal box response (R_G). By association this becomes conditioned to the stimuli in the goal box. It is a well established principle of conditioning that stimuli similar to a conditioned stimulus will to some extent elicit the conditioned response. This is known as 'stimulus generalization'. Spence made use of this principle to state that fractional aspects of the goal response are elicited further back in a maze, where stimuli are perceived as more or less similar to the goal box. These environmentally elicited responses he termed 'fractional anticipatory goal responses' (r_gs for short). These responses may have overt components such as licking the lips, but the point is that they anticipate the goal. From here Spence goes on to say that these responses have their own feedback – r_g gives rise to s_g – and it is these internal stimuli which act as motivators. Such stimuli depend ultimately for their strength on the incentive in the goal box. Spence saw this source of stimulation and motivation, arising from incentive factors, as adding to the stimulation and motivation arising from the drive. Performance, then, was a function of habit (H) multiplied by a combined motivational factor ($D + K$) where K stands for incentive and for Kenneth Spence, the man responsible for integrating incentive effects and Hullian theory. Spence's modification seems quite neat. There is no need to see incentive as 'knowledge of future consequences' pulling a knowledgeable animal to a known-about reward. Instead, we are invited to picture the conditioning of yet more numerous intense stimuli, acting quite mechanistically and causatively to push the animal forward to its destination. But Spence's solution may be more apparent than real, since in practice it is not so easy to separate the two variables 'D' and 'K'. If that is the case might it not be possible and parsimonious to get rid of the original 'D' variable? Can we get rid of drive as a concept altogether?

Pure incentive theory

Drive has been retained as a concept so far because whatever added motivation may be inferred from the environment, we have assumed that there is a basic drive force, stemming usually from the needs of the organism, which push it into activity irrespective of environmental conditions. However the assumption that drive automatically leads to activity has been seriously challenged.

Birch, Burnstein, and Clark (1958) carried out an experiment whereby they fed rats from birth at fixed time intervals, so that the animals got accustomed to being fed at a certain time. When after this prolonged training they were food deprived, Birch *et al.* found that their activity was not related to actual hours of deprivation (the usual measure of drive) but to the times they were 'expecting' to be fed. Whether one says that this activity is mediated by expectations or by fractional anticipatory responses does not matter very much; the important point is that drive does not find much of a place in the scheme of things. The experiment is not without its criticisms. It is perfectly possible to speculate that the activity which normally would have accompanied increased drive has been extinguished during training – the animals, in other words, might already have learned that activity between meals brings no reward. But in practice we can assume that activity is never just a function of deprivation. Why then do we not go on to say that deprivation effects, such as they are, have their effect by increasing the value of the incentive? This, indeed, is the position adopted by incentive theorists such as Bindra (1969), who believe that physiological factors and external stimulation combine to create a Central Motive State. This CMS is quite capable, through association, of being aroused by environmental stimuli, which are more or less related to goal box stimuli. Thus initially neutral stimuli can become *secondary incentives*, as it were, and can mediate long chains of purposeful behaviour.

Mendelson (1966) performed a rather ingenious experiment to try and judge between the predictions of drive theory and incentive theory. He made use of direct brain stimulation in order to 'turn on' hunger in otherwise satiated animals. Some animals were satiated in the maze but hunger was turned on in the goal box and the animals could eat. Other animals experienced the opposite. Hunger was present throughout the maze, and was turned off in the goal box. Drive theory predicts that the animal is pushed into activity and the final outcome is not relevant, from a motivational point of view. Incentive theory on the other hand makes quite the opposite prediction – the outcome is all important since motivation is the 'pull' of the incentive. Mendelson's experiment favoured incentive theory in so far as animals whose hunger was turned off in the goal performed only at chance, despite their hypothesized drive. Animals without drive in the maze, but with an incentive at the end, ran the maze without any problems. The conclusion is that if electrical brain stimulation can be said to be equivalent to deprivation-induced hunger then a drive theory is not supported.

The crucial role that external factors play in the motivation of behaviour does not mean that cognition or knowledge of such factors is equally crucial. It is true that we have got very near to saying 'expectancy' (or something like it) exists in our simpler animal subjects, but even in man behaviour can sometimes be shaped and motivated with little or no awareness. Just by rewarding bits of behaviour with attention or a verbal response such as 'uh-hmm' one can increase the probability of those behaviours occurring again. It helps considerably if a person knows what behaviour brings reward but it is quite possible for their behaviour to be shaped gradually and unknowingly by positive consequences. Keehn (1969) performed a fairly celebrated experiment in which he gave subjects monetary reward for an increase of eye blinking. The cover for the experiment was such that the subjects never knew that the reward was actually contingent on eye blinks. Nevertheless subjects showed an increase of blink rate during the experiment.

The gist of the matter is that there may be no more to motivation than reinforcement. The environment provides stimuli which elicit responses. Those which are reinforced will be elicited next time in the same situation. This is quite a departure from Hull's view where motivation and reinforcement are quite different. Reinforcement, for Hull, was just a matter of cementing habits – it affected *learning*. *Performance* depended on drive. But the experiments we have recently described have broken down that distinction. Reward affects learning, but it also affects performance. For one man this is nothing new. B. F. Skinner had never subscribed to the Hullian drive theory and during all the years which we have considered so far addressed himself to practical questions about the effects of different patterns (or schedules) of reinforcement, on behaviour (see A3). He found radically different behaviour depending on whether it was being rewarded on a time basis or according to response rate, according to fixed schedules or variable ones. For Skinner motivation has never been a problem. Behaviour occurs which is reinforced. But having got rid of drive and put all our eggs in the reinforcement basket so to speak, the reader may well be aware of the next problem. What defines a reinforcer? We, surely, cannot now answer: drive reduction.

What about reduction of internal intense and aversive stimuli? After all, that was the position Miller adopted and the embarrassment of the drive concept does not necessarily invalidate it. The trouble is other findings do. Animals will often work for increases of stimulation. Sheffield *et al.* (1951) showed that rats will learn sequences of behaviour in order to copulate, even when ejaculation is prevented – hardly the most stimulus-reducing activity. If we were asked to say in common-sense terms what the nature of reinforcement is, one might well reply an end result involving pleasure. Now this was a view which remained suspect in early years simply because 'pleasure' seemed a totally mentalistic concept. However recent work in the area of electrical brain stimulation has located what appear to be 'pleasure centres' (see A2). Olds and Milner (1954) showed that there were areas of the brain for the stimulation of which rats would perform responses (such as bar pressing). Of particular importance for a reinforcement view of motivation is that those areas of the hypothalamus which were associated with the onset of activities such as eating, drinking, and sexual behaviour were also areas where rats sought electrical self-stimulation. At a physiological level, therefore, it seems that motivation (what induces behaviour) and reinforcement (what follows the behaviour) are identical.

A reinforcement theorist who asks what motivates behaviour is really asking something about the past reinforcement history of the behaving organism. Motivation has become totally a question of looking at the external determinants of behaviour. The question of internal drives has become redundant.

But we cannot so easily relegate the importance of the intervening organism. It is true that we may sometimes be shaped unawares by the external stimuli which make up our environment. However it is also true that for the most part we have awareness; we also react to the external world *as we perceive it*. This is a suitable point to look at cognitive approaches to the study of motivation.

Summary

1 Mechanistic psychologists, interested in the most parsimonious approach to the explanation of behaviour, evolved a theory which viewed all behaviour as a function of drive (deriving ultimately from biological needs) and habit. Drive pushes an organism blindly into action. Habits are built up by contiguity of response to reinforcement (drive reduction).

2 The variety of behaviour (particularly human behaviour) can be fitted into simple drive theory by postulating acquired reinforcement and acquired drive. Of crucial

explanatory importance is the 'master' acquired drive of fear.

3 There is a gigantic experimental literature which supports many of the postulates and predictions of drive theory. Some experiments on the non-specificity of drive, the predictions about conflict behaviour and verbal learning have been described.

4 Drive theory's first major challenge came with the emergence of incentives as motivational variables. Modifications of the theory were possible, but the modifications only served to increase doubt as to whether drive was necessary at all as a motivational entity. The effect of the usual drive-induction procedures such as deprivation might merely be to increase the value of the incentive. In short, incentive motivation may be the whole story.

5 Incentives do not necessarily have to be thought of as things which are 'known about'. Operationally incentives are reinforcers. Reinforcement and motivation can be seen as identical. But the question then arises as to what is the nature of reinforcement if it is not drive reduction. Hedonistic theories of reinforcement (i.e. the notion that what reinforces is pleasure) have become tenable in so far as physiological evidence shows the existence of so-called 'pleasure centres'. Such pleasure centres are anatomically related to motivational centres thus further supporting the view that reinforcement somehow equals motivation.

6 If external reinforcement is the answer to questions of motivation, we have still got to consider the intervening organism which interprets the external world. We react to interpreted stimuli.

5
Cognitive approaches to motivation

Whilst we have seen that some psychologists have taken as their starting point the denial of cognitive factors in explaining the motivation of behaviour, subscribing as they did to a strong form of Lloyd Morgan's canon, we have also seen that there have been psychologists, even in the early days, who have been willing to consider what goes on 'in the head' of the behaving organism. We mentioned in Chapter 4 that one of Hull's most celebrated opponents was Tolman. Whereas Hull, and his followers, thought of learning and motivation solely in terms of the mapping of stimuli to responses, Tolman believed that it was important to recognize the intervening organism. Whereas systems such as Hull's have been fairly called 'psychologies of the empty organism', Tolman's organism is kept busy. In his view, there is no automatic stamping in of stimulus-response connexions. When, for example, an animal learns a maze, the conceptualization is not (as it is in Hull's system) one of a simple machine being pushed by internally and externally derived forces into a sequence of responses ending up in the goal box; rather the animal acquires information in the form of seeing how stimuli tend to go together (the animal learns, in other words, *S–S* connexions rather than *S–R* ones). Since Tolman's organism is allowed to have something at least approximating to knowledge or expectancy, the question of motivation and reinforcement is put into a quite different perspective. Animals can 'know about' future consequences. Reinforcement, such as food at the end of a maze, does not stamp in habits. The presence of food, along with the features of the maze itself, is something the animal finds out about, and is independent of the learning process. Reinforcement, on this view, is not necessary for learning to occur. Reinforcement is totally a performance variable. Tolman, then, is among the first cognitive theorists.

Both Hull and Tolman, for all their differences, were essentially animal experimenters, devising broad theoretical systems for the analysis of behaviour. However not all psychologists have come to a consideration of motivation from this perspective. Kurt Lewin is in an altogether different tradition.

Lewin's background lay in the Gestalt school of psychology. This tradition had grown up in Germany, under the leadership of men such as Wertheimer, Koffka, and Kohler (see A4). The simple adage that the whole is greater than the sum of its parts lay at the heart of Gestalt psychology. The force of this adage is most clearly pertinent in the gestaltist analysis of perceptual phenomena. Indeed, the beginning of Gestalt psychology is usually dated as 1912, when Wertheimer published his paper on the phi-phenomenon. The phi-phenomenon illustrates very well the principle of the whole being greater than the sum of its parts. When two lights are close together, and are flashed on and off in such a way that the offset of one light immediately accompanies the onset of the other light, the perception is one of apparent movement. The whole effect (that of movement) is not to be found in the parts that make up the demonstration. This historically prior interest in perception carried over to gestaltist interest in the field of learning. Kohler (1925) demonstrated so called 'insight' learning in apes. The animals were seen to solve certain problems not by trial and error, but by sitting and 'thinking' about a possible solution. The gestaltists explained such learning in terms of perceptual reorganization. The discriminated parts of the visual field were reshuffled to form a different whole arrangement which contained a solution to the problem.

Much influenced by the Gestalt psychologists, Lewin adopted many of their terms in his theory of behaviour. He spoke of fields made up of parts. He spoke of the reorganization of fields. He also took up another point: that there is such a thing as subjective perception. There is a difference between the real world and the perceived world. As we shall see, this point is vital to an appreciation of Lewin's thinking.

Lewin believed that behaviour is a joint function of the environment and the person. He expressed this in mathematical notation as: $B = f(P, E)$. Note that this is a far cry from the psychology of the empty organism, with its total reliance on stimuli pushing the organism into activity. Motivation for Lewin depended on how the person perceives the state of affairs which influences his behaviour, and the perceived state of affairs does not always truly reflect the real situation. If the reader were to help a blind man across the road, he might be a little annoyed if the man, white stick in hand, were afterwards to tell him that he were not in fact blind. The motive for such helping behaviour was the man's 'blindness', but that had never existed in the real world; but thanks to the white stick and other cues the 'blind' man had existed in the world of subjective perception. Subjective perception determines the action, and subjective perception is a function of both the environment and the person.

It is not intended here to give any full account of Lewin's whole theory, as our interest is mainly historical. Lewin must be considered a primary front-runner in tracing the traditions of a cognitive psychology of motivation. What we have said so far already illustrates the most important challenge any cognitivist can deliver to a mechanistic theorist of the Hullian kind. Basically, the challenge consists of driving a wedge between those stimuli, external such as food, or internal such as hunger pangs, and the perception of those stimuli. One does not thereby deny that such stimulation plays a very important role in determining behaviour. What the cognitivist wants to deny is that the effect of these stimuli on behaviour is automatic, and thus to make a mechanistic *S–R* psychology untenable.

Nevertheless there are similarities with Hullian theory if only because Lewin, like Hull, was concerned with building up a system to explain behaviour.

The three determinants of performance in Hull's final system were drive, incentive, and habit. Lewin, too, wished to have a system with variables which could interact and give rise to general predictions. Thus he saw behaviour as a multiplicative function of *tension* in parts of the 'field' which makes up a person, of the *valence* or perceived value of the goal object, and of the *psychological distance* from the goal. These echo respectively drive, incentive, and habit. Food deprivation, for example, gives rise to tension in certain parts of the field. If a chocolate cake is available in the person's environment at that moment it will be endowed with positive valence. It only requires that the psychological distance is such that the cake really is available, and the behaviour of grabbing the cake and eating it will be initiated. Note the word 'psychological' before 'distance'. If the person is tied up so he cannot move, the cake which is only inches away in reality, may, psychologically, just as well be at infinity.

We can see then the similarities with Hull's system. Tension is similar to drive, the goal box has valence which is similar to incentive value. The person is psychologically distanced from the goal and is required to use previously learned behaviour to bridge that distance – habits to acquire the goal object are necessary.

The real difference between Lewin and Hull centres on their use of terms. Just as the $r_g - s_g$ mechanism of Chapter 4 could virtually be called expectancy, so Lewin's terms can be used to rephrase the explanation of many of Hull's experiments with rats in mazes. The other difference between Hull and Lewin is their preference for different kinds of empirical data. Lewin prefers to discuss the application of his theory to human behaviour and often relies on anecdotal examples of his theory being applied. Hullians preferred, initially anyway, to work at very precise prediction of circumscribed problem-solving behaviour mainly in infra-human species. There is no doubt that Hull will be remembered as the more important figure of the two, but Lewin's perpetual glance at the motivation of human behaviour served as a useful preamble to more contemporary studies of human motives. It is to these that we now turn.

A motive for achievement

Drive theory, we saw, stressed the importance of aversive stimuli, whether arising from food deprivation or electric shock or whatever, in energizing behaviour. In so far as goal objects diminished these 'drive' stimuli, they reinforced behaviour. Other human motives, however diverse, are in principle to be derived from primary organismic needs. However if we accept the kind of hedonistic view of motivation advanced in the final part of Chapter 4, the question of the derivation of motives becomes less important. It is possible to choose, in a heuristic sort of way, a particular motive, which appears to offer a certain degree of explanatory potential, and pursue one's research from this starting-point. This was very much the approach of a psychologist called McClelland. Among the motives most studied by McClelland was the peculiarly human striving for achievement (see D3). Whether we are talking about striving for success in work situations, or in personal and social relationships, it is noticeable that some of us succeed more than others. McClelland thought that what was common to all these different situations was competition in the presence of an acknowledged standard of excellence.

In order for *achievement motivation* to have any explanatory power in the prediction of human behaviour, it was first necessary to measure it. If that proved possible, a whole field of experimentation could be opened up, which would not be possible using such primordial motivations as hunger. Now, it is no use using past achievement itself as a criterion for the existence of the motive – that would be about as explanatory as saying one cannot sleep because of insomnia. Rather, what is required is some independent means of measuring the assumed motive of achievement, antecedent to an observation of actual achievement behaviour.

The measurement of achievement motivation

If the need for achievement exists prior to actual achievement behaviour we should expect, perhaps, that it might pervade in some way the person's thinking and their fantasy life. If we can somehow tap the contents of these private meanderings, we could perhaps begin to make a judgement about how achievement motivated a person is. Workers in the field of achievement motivation have done this by using a personality test known as the Thematic Apperception Test (TAT) (see D3 and E2). The TAT is known as a *projective* test in that the person is shown ambiguous stimuli and in describing them is thought to project elements of his own personality into his descriptions. Readers may well be aware of the other major projective test: the Rorschach or ink-blot test. In that test, since the only thing that really exists is an ink-blot, any further descriptive elaboration should tell us something about the person doing the describing. The TAT consists of pictures which the person is invited to weave into a story. He is asked to describe what led up to the scene depicted, what is happening in the picture, and what the outcome of it all will be. Murray, who devised the test, guessed that in writing the story the subject would, because of the ambiguities in the situations presented, be forced to project into the story some of his own fantasy material.

By analysing the content of the stories, it is possible to score them for the degree of achievement motivation they show.

Reliability and validity of the measures

McClelland *et al.* (1953) offer a certain amount of evidence to show that measures of achievement motivation (called nAch for short) are meaningful. Certainly independent judges who score the same TAT records tend to agree surprisingly well – the inter-rater reliability, in other words, is quite adequate. However when groups of subjects are retested after a fairly long period of time the correlations, though significant, tend to be lower – test-retest reliability is not so good.

Lowell (1952) demonstrated the criterion validity of the TAT measure. (Criterion validity centres on the question of whether the measures satisfy the obvious criterion of differentiating between actual high and low achievers.) He showed that high achievers as measured by TAT did better than low achievers when they were presented with an anagram solving task. Atkinson (1953) investigated the recall of items in a task, after subjecting his experimental subjects to three sets of instructions, designed to arouse low, middling, and high amounts of achievement motivation. Recall was enhanced for those classified as high achievers in the achievement-oriented condition. The opposite was the case for those classified as low achievers, who did better when the instructions were relaxed and did not arouse achievement motivation. French and Thomas (1958) gave subjects an insoluble task and measured the persistence of subjects in trying to find a solution. High achievers were found to show more perseverance. Lastly, Mischel (1961) showed that high achievement motivated children were more likely to delay immediate reward in order to achieve a delayed but superior reward.

nAch as a valid measure has extended itself beyond the kind of laboratory experiments mentioned above. By analysing the literary work of different societies and the same societies at different times, McClelland has shown a relationship between judgements of nAch from such material and various indices of economic achievement. McClelland (1961), for example, gives data which relates the nAch of various countries to electrical output in the post-war years. Other hypotheses which have been supported are that Protestant countries show greater nAch and economic performance than Catholic countries, and that levels of achievement motivation, assessed by analysis of literature, are related to periods in a country's history of strong economic growth. McClelland and his collaborators have also shown that rises in nAch tend to precede such periods of growth by a small amount.

These sorts of finding suggest that nAch might be a very important consideration when we look at the future of our own societies. More recently McClelland *et al.* (1969) have been investigating whether increased nAch can be taught. Using intensive training courses they have tried to train people in achievement-related behaviours and claim some success.

However we should not be carried away with too much enthusiasm. Apart from fundamental questions about the desirability of conventionally achievement-oriented societies, there are more specific criticisms of McClelland's work. The kind of training programmes are so arranged in terms of teaching a variety of skills that any number of factors might be responsible for observed changes. There is no evidence as yet to suppose that any changes which do occur have a relatively permanent effect on the nAch scores of the trainees. There is no doubt however that nAch has given rise, and continues to give rise, to a considerable literature of experiments. Moreover there have been attempts to integrate work on the achievement motive into a broader behaviour theory. We now turn to one of the most important of these.

Atkinson's system

The most comprehensive attempt to build up a theory of behaviour using the motive of achievement is associated with the psychologist Atkinson. He believed that three variables were important in the arousal of nAch and consequent performance. These variables were the actual level of nAch of the subject, his expectancies (measured in terms of probability of success), and the pay-off or incentive value of the outcome. Already we can see again, as we did in the case of Lewin, that there are similarities to Hull's system. The motivational term of nAch corresponds with drive, expectancy corresponds with the notion of habit strength, whilst incentive is common to both systems.

Atkinson, however, was also responsible for introducing another aspect into his system. He believed that achievement-related tasks elicited not only positive affective anticipations (a motive to approach the task and succeed) but also a negative affective anticipation (a motive to avoid the task). The latter may be deemed *fear of failure* (FF).

As a result of past experience and individual differences, people bring different balances of these two motives into a situation. Performance is thus seen as a function of the interaction of both these motivations. By these means, Atkinson made the predictive power of the original theory that much greater. In general an individual's performance will be as follows, in achievement-related situations: the total tendency to approach (a product of all three variables associated with success) *minus* the total tendency to avoid (a product of fear of failure motivation, and the expectancies and outcomes associated with failure). This formulation gives rise to certain quite specific predictions, when one compares subjects who are high in nAch and low in FF with subjects who are high in FF and low in nAch. The former are expected to be more realistic in the level of difficulty they choose for a task. The reason is quite simple. They will not choose extremely difficult tasks where the probability of success is so small as to be unrealistic, since they are motivated to achieve. Contrarily they will not choose tasks which are too easy for them, because, though the probability of success is very high, the incentive is very small (incentive and probability of success are of course interdependent: Incentive $= 1 - P$ [success]). In consequence their motive for achievement is maximally aroused in tasks of intermediate difficulty (i.e. where P (success) $= 0{\cdot}5$). Now let us consider the person whose fear of failure is greater than their achievement motivation. Here we should expect the opposite to hold true. Tasks of intermediate difficulty arouse the most anxiety. If the task is very simple and the probability of failure is small then there are no problems. Paradoxically, if the task is extremely difficult, there are no problems either, since the negative incentive of failing is not great. The present writer is reminded of a car driver who held up a whole queue of traffic by his inability to overtake a crawling juggernaut. Obviously aware that the task was to overtake (he presumably did not wish to travel the breadth of the British Isles at such a speed), he made many futile attempts to overtake when it was clearly not advisable. The probability of success being very small, his negative incentive for having failed was minute. Ignoring intermediate chances, which clearly would have been successful, he eventually chose to overtake when the oncoming traffic lane looked like a runway cleared for take-off. No doubt the reader can think of his own examples of Atkinson's model in operation.

Experiments which have studied risk-taking behaviour in the laboratory have borne out the view that those high in nAch do choose tasks of intermediate difficulty more consistently than either those low in such motivation, or those who are relatively higher in motivation arising from fear of failure. Atkinson and Litwin (1960) involved subjects in a game which consisted of throwing rings on to pegs. Subjects could stand at varying distances from the target. Results showed that subjects high in nAch and low in FF motivation were much more consistent in their tendency to stand around a middling distance from the target.

Feather (1961) went far in demonstrating the utility of Atkinson's model, when he investigated the extent to which subjects differing in balance of nAch and FF also differed in their willingness to persist at a task after a failure experience. In brief, subjects high in nAch and relatively lower in FF would be expected to persevere at an easy task, if they failed. The reason for such a prediction is that the subject would reassess the difficulty of the task after the failure experience – it would be seen as not so easy after all, and more as an intermediately difficult task. If the original task was presented to the subjects as fairly difficult to start off with, then one makes contrary predictions. Here, the reassessment upgrades the difficulty of the task still further and the perceived probability of success is not good enough to engage fully the nAch of the subjects. Persistence in this latter circumstance is not to be expected. Now let us look at the situations as they affect the person high in FF and relatively low in nAch. If the situation is first presented as involving an easy solution then a failure experience will once again induce a reassessment towards the task being of intermediate difficulty. We have seen already that this is the sort of task that the high FF subject wants most to avoid, because the negative incentive of failure is at its greatest. Paradoxically when the subject fails at a task which is first presented as quite difficult, he should have no trouble in persisting at it, because he reassesses it as more difficult and thus the 'shame' of failing is lessened.

Feather went about testing these predictions by using a task of tracing around a figure without removing the pen from the paper. The task of course, in reality, was an impossible one, since it was necessary to induce failure experiences in all of his subjects. He manipulated his subjects' initial perceived probability of success by presenting them with false norms. The predictions of Atkinson's theory were, in fact, confirmed.

It is not difficult to see that Atkinson's theory could be of great importance in the field of education. For example, we may well ask whether achievement motivation plays an important role in determining the wisdom of career choices among students. Mahone (1960) confirmed predictions derived from the model we have just been discussing. He expected that students in whom nAch was relatively greater than FF would be more realistic in their career choices, avoiding over-ambitious projects with unrealistic probabilities of success. Likewise they would avoid too easy career choices, since they would not offer sufficient positive incentive. Students who were high in FF and relatively low in nAch would be expected either to keep their career choices somewhat uninspiring (in order to minimize the threat of keen competition) or alternatively to aim for something quite beyond their capabilities with the likelihood of failing (such failure, in the circumstances, being unlikely to evoke too much negative reaction, and quite likely even to evoke positive reinforcement of the kind: 'Well, at least he's a good trier.'). Mahone's survey of nAch, FF, and career choices among students confirmed these predictions of Atkinson's model.

Achievement motivation continues to be a concept capable of giving rise to greater and greater experimentation and application. But the cognitive psychology of motivation has at the same time moved further inside the subject, if we may be allowed to use such a term, and we shall now consider some work by psychologists which suggest that it is not enough simply to invoke a motive and use it as a variable in a behavioural model. The crux of cognition is that it implies the organism has to *interpret* its inner states before they can be truly seen as determinants of behaviour.

When we considered the humble rat we were forced, albeit grudgingly, to give it a limited sort of cognition in terms of expectancy, or at least 'anticipatory responses'. However the environment of that creature tended to consist of expected food pellets or electric shocks. Man's environment most of all is a *social* environment. It is no surprise therefore to realize that social factors have a profound bearing on an individual's motives for behaving.

The environment and the interpretation of motive states

Whatever the derivation of our motives, we have seen that it is possible to see motivation in general as being concerned with the seeking of pleasure and the avoidance of pain – the so called hedonistic theory. Our awareness of motives therefore has an affective quality and this quality we tend to label as an *emotion* (a word which the reader will no doubt realize has a common root with the word motivation). But the question arises: are these emotions, which we feel, completely laid down in our physiology, or are they things which we infer on the basis of information from internal and external sources?

Schachter and Singer (1962) undertook some ingenious research to show that people labelled their emotions on the basis of information present in the social environment. In one part of their experiment they injected some of their subjects with a drug called epinephrine (or adrenalin), which has the effect of inducing heightened physiological arousal. For control purposes other subjects were simply injected with ordinary saline solution. Subjects were then placed in one of two social situations. Either they would be placed in the company of a stooge – a confederate of the experimenter – who behaved in a somewhat euphoric and manic fashion. Alternatively, and once again with a stooge, they were asked to fill in a probing questionnaire. The stooge had instructions to react to the situation by behaving very angrily. Schachter and Singer found that subjects in the first condition took their cue from the stooge and interpreted their drug-induced emotion as euphoria. Subjects in the second condition interpreted their emotion as anger and aggressiveness. Both groups of subjects exhibited these tendencies to a much larger degree than the control subjects who had only received the injection of salt solution.

The message of this experiment, as well as a number of subsequent experiments by Schachter and his colleagues, is that the labelling of emotions is an interaction between physiological arousal and the social context of the environment in which the individual finds himself. This, naturally, is an important finding. The whole question of this book has been what determines behaviour, and the answer in some sense has been a motive. We now find that the motive itself does not exist in isolation; rather it is given meaning, and therefore a propensity for certain behaviour, by the social environment.

However it is possible to argue that the internal cues, as well as the external ones, have also to go through the process of cognition. Internal stimuli, like external ones, can be denied, distorted, or alternatively exaggerated. This is the position adopted by Valins (1966). In order to support this position, Valins and his co-researchers have done a series of experiments utilizing false feedback about internal arousal cues. Valins (1966) got male students to look at colour slides of scantily clad females. Whilst they were doing this they were told that they would hear the feedback from their own heart beats. In fact, Valins arranged that the feedback be false. After the showing of the slides, subjects were asked to rate them for attractiveness. The main result, shown by Valins' study, was that those slides which had been accompanied by seemingly increased heart rate were judged more attractive. Valins concludes that the 'truth' of the internal state is not what is important, it is the cognition of it which interacts with the social environment to result in a labelled emotion.

Valins and Ray (1967) addressed themselves to that motive state of fear, so dear to the hearts of drive theorists. By manipulating heart rate feedback, they managed to convince fearful subjects that they were becoming less afraid of snakes, when pictures of these were presented.

Since fear tends to motivate avoidance, this kind of work has definite implications for the modification of irrational fears. Theoretically at least, it should now be possible to drive a logical wedge between the 'physiological fear' elicited by a phobic object and the 'cognitive fear' on which the decision to avoid is presumably based. The present author is at the moment investigating whether by suitable instructions subjects, afraid of spiders, can be induced to alter their cognition of fear. Paradoxically they are told that they *will* be afraid when they encounter the spider, but are persuaded that fear is not something to be afraid of. The assumption lying behind the research is that subjects avoid spiders because they are suffering from a fear of fear. Preliminary results indicate that suitable instructions can have a significant effect in reducing avoidance responding in the presence of a live spider. The fear drive of the last chapter seems then not to be a unitary concept, and it seems reasonable to consider physiological, behavioural, and verbal measures of it as separate but interacting (see Lang, 1968).

In the above scheme of things, fear as a motivator is effectively denied. Fear, as indicated by any of the various measures usually employed – heart rate, verbal report, or avoidance behaviour – is simply a collection of responses. These responses and the stimuli associated with them are simply grist for the mill which produces the final cognition. And it is the cognition which is the ultimate motive source. This is a view which is currently associated with psychologists such as R. S. Lazarus (1968).

The usual experimental design used by Lazarus and his associates (see Lazarus and Opton, 1966) is to show a stress-inducing film (e.g. circumcision practices in primitive societies), monitor physiological stress reactions in experimental subjects viewing the film, and then to reduce such reactions by accompanying cues designed either to cause denial of stress, or intellectualization of it. The conclusion that Lazarus comes to is very clear: emotional reactions stem from cognitions.

Cognitive dissonance

Once we recognize the importance of cognitions in guiding behaviour, we are forced to look at the *totality* of cognitions as they exist for an individual in his social environment. We then cannot but realize that cognitions can be in conflict. Some of us smoke cigarettes – that is a cognition of which we are directly aware. Those of us who smoke cigarettes also know that there is a link between cigarette smoking and lung cancer – a cognition we are made aware of through the media. Now assuming that we are not deliberately trying to kill ourselves when we smoke, it is immediately apparent that we have two cognitions which are in conflict. Certain psychologists have suggested that dissonance between cognitions is a very powerful source of motivation in everyday life (see B1 and B3). An individual, in becoming aware of cognitive dissonance, will strive to reduce it. If we say the individual is striving for a balance between his cognitions, we can see that there are similarities to the ideas of homeostasis which we mentioned in connexion with physiological mechanisms underlying primary biological motivations.

The celebrated name in the area of cognitive dissonance research is Festinger. He has done a number of experiments where he has established the existence of cognitive dissonance and gone on to predict the various self-justifications which tend to resolve it. For example, in the case of dissonance deriving from smoking behaviour, he predicted and found that smokers were much more likely to question the validity of the cancer research findings than non-smokers.

Festinger and Carlsmith (1959) got subjects to participate in a very boring experiment. Some subjects were only given a small reward for their participation, whilst other subjects were given an extremely large reward. Festinger argued that the small reward would not be seen as adequate recompense for participation in a very boring experiment, and this would give rise to a state of cognitive dissonance. Since the dissonance could not be solved by altering the reward – the experiment was now over – the subjects could only resolve their dissonance by altering their cognition of the experiment. It was predicted that the subjects given the small reward would say that the experiment was not really as boring as all that. Subjects given the large reward would not have any dissonance aroused and would thus be quite content to see the experiment as boring as it had been previously described. On post-experiment ratings the expected differences between the two groups of subjects (when asked to rate the experiment for its 'boringness') were in fact found.

Aronson and Carlsmith (1963) showed that the resolution of cognitive dissonance can have the opposite effect of reducing the attractiveness of a situation. They prevented children from playing with obviously attractive toys by either issuing a mild threat of punishment or a severe threat. It was predicted that the mild threat would create more cognitive dissonance and lead the children to think along the following line: 'why am I not playing with these very attractive toys when the punishment associated with doing so is not all that great?' The answer to such a question and thus the resolution of dissonance is to conclude that the toys really are not that attractive anyway. Those children who are threatened severely have no dissonance. The toys remain attractive and the threat of punishment is reason enough to suppress the behaviour of playing with them. Aronson and Carlsmith's predictions were confirmed. This experiment is very relevant to a consideration of how a pro-social conscience might be shaped in children. Use of severe sanctions is likely to suppress anti-social behaviour only in certain prescribed situations (e.g. when the parents are present) and is not likely to lead to any internalized means of self control. More subtle use of sanctions, on the other hand, could facilitate self-controlled pro-social behaviour – the exercise of conscience, in other words. Work on the relation of anti-social behaviour and parental style of upbringing would seem to support this line of thinking (see Bandura, 1969).

Cognitions about internal states are also possible sources of the arousal of dissonance. Brehm (1962) pretended to his subjects that he was investigating the effect of hunger, through food deprivation, on various aspects of performance. Using the same paradigm as Festinger and Carlsmith, he gave some of his subjects a reward for their co-operation, whilst others were given no recompense. Subjects who had received no reward subsequently reported less hunger than their counterparts. Brehm argues that the no-reward condition induces a state of dissonance which is resolved by minimizing the discomfiture which is being inflicted. Brehm also replicated the finding using thirst as the dependent variable.

Our conclusions must be that cognitions determine behaviour to a very large extent. In the last experiment by Brehm we see that even the biological motives we began with have still to be interpreted by the individual before they are truly labelled 'hunger' or 'thirst' – and thus presumably give rise to a need to eat or to drink. Cognitive dissonance paradigms have been vital in illuminating this particular issue. Normally, of course, hunger and thirst, if acute, would behave in just the kind of primary biological drive sort of way that we began by considering. But now instead of thinking of them as blind drive, we should see them as sources of information which, if acute, will be of over-riding importance. If, however, they are not acute they will just be additional sources of information which the organism takes into account in deciding its behaviour.

Other motives

Do we have motives to conform, to affiliate with one another, to depend on one another, to aggress amongst ourselves? The answer is probably yes, in the very obvious sense that we all to some extent are conformist, affiliative, dependent, and aggressive. If motivation is rooted in reinforcement, the degree that we show these motives is naturally itself rooted in our reinforcement histories, as well as being elicited by information from cues in the environment. The aim of this book is, however, a theoretical one, and space does not permit a discussion of detailed experiments pertaining to any and every social motive of individuals, living in a 'shaping' society. One hopes rather that the reader will by now have a general view of motivation as it has developed in psychology from the picture of an organism being pushed around by forces and habits to the alternative picture of an organism, capable within the limitations of its species, of taking in information from its internal physiology, its physical environment, and, most of all in man, its social environment. Only then will reinforcement 'scientifically' steer us to what we expect on the basis of all the information we have culled (rightly or wrongly) or denied (rightly or wrongly). Of course sometimes reinforcement determines our behaviour without awareness – remember the experiment by Keehn. However we cannot fail to be aware that in general we *are* aware when it comes to saying why we do things. Lloyd Morgan's canon, quoted at the beginning of Chapter 4, warned us against invoking reasons, intentions, and purposes in a psychology of motivation. They now perhaps can be readmitted into court, because usually they point all too clearly to the end result of the behaviour – the reinforcer.

Summary

1 Tolman's work is contrasted with that of Hull. It is evident straightway that Tolman is willing to attribute cognition to his organism. Nevertheless Tolman, like Hull, was concerned essentially with animal experimentation, and cognition never really went further than an acknowledged 'expectation' of reinforcement in the goal box.

2 Lewin, in contrast to Tolman, was essentially concerned

with building up a system to explain human behaviour. He thought of behaviour as a function of the person and the environment: $B = f(P, E)$. Lewin's system, though illuminating as an early cognitive endeavour, never gave rise to very precise experimentation and relied heavily on anecdotal examples of its *modus operandi*.

3 McClelland's motive for achievement is taken as a good example of something which is reasonably measurable and which can, in addition, lead to predictions about behaviour in situations inside and outside the laboratory. Atkinson's system, which combines achievement motivation and fear of failure is described, and experiments are outlined which testify to its utility.

4 The cognitive theories so far described still remain close to theories such as Hull's in so far as they see behaviour as a multiplicative function of specific variables: something like motive, expectation, and incentive, allowing for preferences in terminology, are common to all theories. Recent work is described which shows that motives have to be interpreted before they acquire a certain label, which in turn, of course, delineates appropriate behaviour. Schachter thinks of motives arising from environmental information interacting with internal states of physiological arousal. Valins and others have stated that even information from one's physiology is subject to the same process of cognitive interpretation. The cognition, after all the necessary interpretation, is the source of motivation.

5 Cognitions can be in conflict. Work is described on cognitive dissonance. The experimental paradigms of Festinger have been useful in showing that even primary motives such as hunger have to be interpreted and assessed before they link up with their natural behavioural consequences such as eating.

6 Obviously other motives are learned in a social context. Their strength varies between individuals according to

reinforcement histories (they will also vary across different societies). The cognitive view of motivation remains the same for these other motives. Cognitions stem from all sources of information and behaviour is guided by reinforcement.

6
Psychoanalysis and the therapeutic tradition

In terms of the sheer number of people who have heard of Freud and his ideas, he is without doubt the most celebrated figure in the whole of psychology (see D3). A simplified view of psychoanalysis is that it is concerned with the unveiling of unconscious motives for much human behaviour, in particular the sort of abnormal behaviour that leads people to seek medical assistance. This in fact is essentially an accurate view. It is thus possible to see psychoanalysis primarily as a psychology of motivation.

Freud was born in Vienna in 1856 and was first trained as a medical practitioner. Although recognized as the founder of psychoanalysis, it is probably more correct to say that psychoanalysis was evolved rather than created. The term psychoanalysis was first used by Freud in a paper he delivered in March 1896. But as Strachey points out in his editorial comments to Freud's famous book *The Interpretation of Dreams* (1900) the foundations of psychoanalysis were laid in earlier days than this, and one must have recourse to his teachers whose influence on Freud's later ideas was without doubt formidable.

Freud's teacher in the early days was one Ernst Brucke, and it was the philosophical approach to medicine which he represented which helped to shape the young Freud. Brucke subscribed to what was known as the Helmholzian school of thought – a reductionist approach which in medicine translated itself into the belief that no forces other than physical-chemical ones were active within the organism. This had both a positive and a negative effect on Freud. Positively, he became and always remained a reductionist. For him behaviour was totally determined, and never did he relinquish his belief that any phenomenon he studied had a cause. Negatively, the reductionist credo seemed to rule out any systematic and scientific approach to the *psychological* problems, with which Freud, as we shall see, became exclusively occupied. Freud was motivated to achieve a synthesis. In turning away from physicalistic reductionism (as a pragmatic consideration certainly) and yet retaining reductionism as a principle *per se*, he evolved the notion of 'psychic determinism' – the idea that there are mental forces which determine mental events. The forces which Freud postulated were, as everyone now knows, 'instincts', or to be more exact instinctual drives (from the German word 'Trieb'). Although the forces deriving from the instincts were assumed to be mental (or psychic representations) it is clear that Freud ultimately wished to ground psychoanalysis, however speculatively, in the firm soil of biology.

The second great influencer of Freud, from a theoretical point of view, was Professor Theodore Meynert, to whose clinic Freud moved in 1883. Meynert taught psychiatry and neurology in a way which emphasized the importance of reflexes and central control by the brain. Moreover Meynert believed that even simple reflexes such as an infant searching for the mother's breast had conscious concomitants, and used the term 'primary ego' to refer to the conscious aspect of the behaving individual. The primary ego of Meynert in many ways foreshadows Freud's own use of the ego, as one of his structures of mind (see below).

The primary aim of Meynert's ego was to reduce pain. This, too, became incorporated into Freud's ideas of a 'pleasure principle' which governs ultimately a person's behaviour. Many other of Freud's later concepts can be seen in Meynert's ideas. Admittedly Meynert used his terms usually in a more physiological context. It was only later that Freud realized the limitations of psychology based on neurological enquiry and thus gave his terms a purely psychological connotation.

If Brucke and Meynert were the main influential precursors of Freudian theory, it is true to say that Josef Breuer and the French physician Charcot were the two figures who helped most to shape the beginnings of psychoanalytic practice.

Unconscious causation

Freud and Breuer had both been pupils at Brucke's physiological institute in the late 1870s. Among the patients that Breuer later became interested in were those classified as hysterics. Such patients, usually women, often suffered with symptoms of paralysis. Now although the symptoms were quite indisputable, the paralysis in such cases could be shown to have no actual neurological cause, and hysterics were thought by many to be malingerers. Breuer had an interest in the technique of hypnosis, and during the period from 1880 to 1882 he used hypnosis in the treatment of a female hysteric with paralysis of the arm. He used to visit his patient, a certain Fraulein Anna O., put her into a hypnotic state, and get her to talk around her symptoms. When this was done the symptoms tended to be relieved. Anna herself referred to this as the 'talking cure'.

From this case Breuer went on to evolve his cathartic method whereby he relieved patients' hysterical, usually paralytic, symptoms while encouraging them to discuss them in the hypnotic state. Meanwhile Freud had obtained a research grant to visit Charcot in Paris and observed there both the elicitation and removal of paralytic symptoms under hypnosis. It occurred to Freud that since hypnosis could induce a complete remission of the symptom, it must be that in the normal state something, of which the patient was not aware, was responsible for maintaining the symptom. The idea was born of symptoms having unconscious causes.

This insight was corroborated by Breuer's finding in the case of Fraulein Anna that the hysterical paralysis of the arm was directly related to a forgotten and traumatic event, surrounding the circumstances of her father's death. Remission of the symptom took place after the event was recalled in the hypnotic state. The discovery of the role of unconscious factors in maintaining specific symptoms was the crucial starting point for psychoanalysis and the pervasive generalization which follows in its wake: that we behave often for reasons of which we are completely unaware.

A dynamic unconscious

Freud did not stay with the practice of hypnosis for very long. It was true that Breuer's method achieved some success, but Freud noticed that the success was often shortlived. He found also that patients started to develop a relationship towards him which appeared infantile and sensual. In so far as treatment terminated this peculiar relationship, the symptoms would return. Also Freud noticed that he could not always induce a workable depth of hypnosis. So instead of hypnosis, he began to use a technique of applying gentle pressure to the patient's forehead and demanding that the patient should say whatever was going on in his mind. Later he abandoned all devices and simply asked the patient to associate freely around whatever was going on in his mind. In abandoning hypnosis Freud was able to see that unconscious material did not simply lie passively waiting to be recovered, but the patient was actively fighting against its release into consciousness. He discovered the phenomenon of resistance. The unconscious was not static; it was dynamic and when resistance weakened it would rise to the surface, so to speak. Freud used everyday behaviours such as slips of the tongue to show how an unconscious intention can catch the person off-guard and realize itself.

Instinctual impulses and sex

Freud's debt to Charcot was no less than his debt to Breuer. That sexual matters lie at the core of neurotic disorders is a view only too well associated with the name of Freud. And yet it seemed that Charcot also had privately come to this belief, and only differed from Freud in his unwillingness to put his views forward in public debate. However it is still clear that the ascendancy which sexual factors gained in the developing Freudian theory was most firmly based in the concrete experience of Freud in treating patients, whose free associative ramblings returned again and again to sexual experiences in childhood. At first, Freud guessed that some real unconscious sexual trauma lay at the root of all neuroses. But it soon became obvious that few, if any, of his patients could really have undergone some of the actual traumas which appeared in their associations. The final stage in the development of the hard core of early Freudian theory was when Freud began to recognize the role of phantasy and projection of phantasy onto memory. It became clear to Freud that sexual impulses lay at the root of many of the symptoms he saw, and that his patients' sexual associations and memories went back right beyond puberty. He was forced to recognize the existence of a real but diffuse sexuality in infancy. It was clear, first, that the experiences 'remembered' by his patients must have been well and truly embellished by phantasy, and secondly, that the primary object of the child's sexual interest and phantasying imagination could not be other than the parents, in particular the parent of the opposite sex. That the young boy should fall in love with his mother, that is the classic Oedipus Complex, became a cornerstone of psychoanalysis.

Freud increasingly came to see much adult human behaviour, normal and abnormal, as the indirect expression of unconscious sexual impulses. We should, however, note that Freud's use of the word 'sexual' meant to convey a rather wider meaning than many of his early critics realized. Infantile sexuality referred to occupation with pleasure experienced in many *erogenous* zones, not just the genitals. Thus sucking in the infant is supposedly in the Freudian scheme of things orally sexual, and since this is a major preoccupation of the child in the very first year of its life, Freud called this the oral stage of development. Later with toilet training the child's focus of attention becomes the anus, and the pleasure associated with movement of the anal sphincter. Thus is heralded the anal stage of development. About the age of four, attention becomes centred on the genitals as a source of pleasure. But also about this age Freud assumed that the child becomes less a bundle of self-centred impulses (he believed that the oral and anal stages were predominantly narcissistic) and more capable of forming strong and erotic attachments to persons other than himself. The age of four, then, also becomes the year of the Oedipus Complex. The young boy falls in love with his mother and becomes jealous of his father. Anxiety supposedly develops for two reasons. First, the boy feels guilty about his hostile feelings for his father, since in most cases there are 'good feelings' as well as bad for him.

Secondly, he fears that he will betray his feelings of hostility and that his father will retaliate. Freud, on the basis of his patients' reported memories, was quite specific about the kind of retaliation the child fears in his darkest phantasies. Given the child's preoccupation with the genitals, and his growing awareness of the difference between males and females, his fear is of castration. Castration appears a terrifying but plausible explanation for the difference between the sexes. Overwhelmed then by the fate that he sees awaiting him, the typical boy according to Freud buries his feelings for his mother in the nether regions of the unconscious, and forms a strong identification with his father.

Now we could go on to detail the importance of the Oedipus Complex to psychoanalysis, we could criticize its supposed universality, or we might wish to defend some wider variant of it, such as a family complex, as suggested by contemporary psychoanalysts such as Guntrip (1964). However in this chapter we must concentrate more or less exclusively on the purely motivational rather than developmental aspects of Freudian psychology, and can therefore only give a cursory account of Freud's psychosexual stages of development. On the motivational side, the importance of infantile sexuality lies in the assumption that the oral, anal, and generally polymorphous sexual impulses of infancy do not disappear, but live on in the unconscious and continue to influence behaviour in the adult. To some extent, the pattern of sexual development allows for a gradual integration into what Freud called mature genital sexuality. But Freud never believed that this took care of all unconscious sexual motivation. Thus forces remained which cried out for expression, and it is necessary now to look at the more indirect ways in which these forces can be dealt with. Before we can do that however, we need to understand the nature of instinctual drive as Freud understood it, and also the structures of mind which he hypothesized as using and channelling the forces of instinct.

Instinctual drive

Freud believed that instinctual drives had three major characteristics: a source, an aim, and an object. Thus hunger had its source in the internal stimulation associated with food deprivation, the aim of the drive is to reduce such stimulation, and objects are sought which satisfy the aroused impulse and result in pleasureable experience. Freud identified all pleasure as being synonymous with a state of quiescence in the nervous system, following some stimulus induced disturbance. Although this was a view compatible with the knowledge of nervous system functioning at that time, it is no longer one which is accepted today. We now know that the nervous system is never quiescent in this way. On the contrary, it is continually active and maintains a general level of activity. Even Freud was aware that behaviourally an organism does not always behave as if it were trying to decrease stimulation. In certain situations, indeed, the organism often seems to be searching for an increase of stimulation. Freud in fact recognized towards the end of his career that some kind of balance or quality of change might be the aim of instinctual drives rather than simply some sort of tension reduction. Note however, even with respect to his early tension-reducing ideas, he is in line with other theorists we have mentioned. We may remember that Hull's formulation was in terms of motivational drive which seeks reduction. Hull's early views also suffered the same embarrassment in the face of experiments and observations which appeared to show that an organism does seek in certain circumstances an increase of stimulation.

Where Freud does part company from other schools of

thought is in the nature of his basic instincts. At first he thought that there were two main classes of instincts: self-preservative ones, hunger being an obvious example; secondly, a broad class of sexual drives whose common energy Freud called *libido.* Through various kinds of channelling concepts which we shall discuss a little later, Freud sought to explain the motivation of much patently non-sexual behaviour by reference to the internal pushing of libidinal forces.

Later Freud tended to put libidinal and self-preservative instincts side by side, and think of them as life forces, or more poetically he called them 'Eros'. Opposing Eros was a class of destructive instincts which Freud called 'Thanatos' or the death instinct. Before this change in his thinking, Freud had conceived of aggressive urges as developing from the thwarting of libidinal forces, but, influenced by the destructive forces he saw unleashed in Europe between 1914 and 1918, he became convinced that the seeds of destruction were innate in man, and that the primary aim of Thanatos was self-destruction: the principle of entropy that the aim of life is death. The death instinct was never so clearly formulated in Freudian theory as the life instincts, but Freud saw its primary feature as a regressive pull on the organism, a retreat into a sort of peaceful non-existence, following what Freud called a Nirvana principle. Through the operation of the pleasure principle the ultimate aims of the death instinct are held in check. Alternatively, the forces of Thanatos can be turned out from the individual and find release in outward displays of aggression against others. Of all Freud's thinking the concept of Thanatos is probably the most speculative and indeed most of his followers and disciples (with the influential exception of Melanie Klein) did not take up this idea very seriously. It would seem fundamentally unverifiable – more so than much else in Freudian theory – and seems to say more about the rather pessimistic personality of Freud than of the phenomena it sought to explain.

Structures of mind

So far we have talked about mind very much as if there is a conscious and unconscious mind, and this does in fact reflect Freud's earliest view. However, he later became dissatisfied with this. The degree of consciousness was a quality attaching to mental events rather than having to do with the structure of mind. It would have been all right if all the instinctual impulses he hypothesized were the stuff of the unconscious, whilst the checking forces were conscious. However this was not how things appeared in his total picture. So in place of the early division, he sectioned the mind into three compartments: *id*, *ego* and *suger-ego*. The *id* was conceptualized as a sort of reservoir of instinctual impulses, seeking gratification, and completely unconscious. In so far as impulses cannot be easily and directly gratified in the external world, Freud believed that the mind evolved an outer structure, the *ego*, which mediated between the primary demands of the id and the not always compatible vicissitudes of the external world. The ego was thought to be largely conscious and perceptual for obvious reasons. However it also, at the unconscious level, has to be in contact with the id. The *super-ego* was invoked by Freud to explain the fact that we tend to internalize attitudes and values from the people around us. We then treat these internalized tendencies as if they were parts of ourselves. The super-ego can be thought of as something resembling a conscience. Certainly the conscious part of the super-ego is virtually synonymous with the term conscience. However the super-ego also spans the layers of consciousness and is assumed to reside partly in unconscious zones. Freud did not seek to determine fixed boundaries for his structures of mind. Rather he assumed that they merged into one another. Indeed it could hardly be otherwise, since he believed that life commences as just one structure: the new-born baby is thought of as simply a bundle of seething instinctual energy – in other words: all id. Because the discharge of energy requires mediation with the world around, the ego evolves from the id. In turn, since the external world is more than just a physically constraining world but a socially constraining one too, there is need to develop yet another structure, namely the super-ego.

As we shall now go on to see, Freud's belief was that human behaviour is simply the surface feature of the individual's struggle to gratify instinctual impulses. The id, ego, and super-ego are involved below the surface in varying degrees of combat about the exact means of gratification.

The dynamics of behaviour

Since the facts of reality dictate that the life of the individual cannot be one eternal orgasmic experience of pleasure, Freudian theory must account for the development and motivation of behaviour as it actually is. Central in Freud's theory is the notion of *displacement*. It will be recollected from Chapter 2 that the ethologists also use the term displacement to refer to the behaviour that is elicited when instinctive patterns are thwarted by conflict. Freud's concept is not dissimilar. The energy or libido deriving from sexual impulses can be channelled independently of a sexual aim or object. Freud conceived that much pro-social behaviour (including the building of civilization itself!) was due to such displacement of libido. This particular kind of channelling he called sublimation. Since it is likely that not all energy will be used up in this way,

Freud thought that the ego itself could 'steal' the excess of energy from the id, and use it to prevent the discharge of further energy from the id. The technical terms he used were *cathexis* and *anticathexis*. The word cathexis describes the outward discharge of energy on to a certain *cathected* object. Anticathexis describes the energy used by the ego in preventing such cathexis.

It is clear, then, that Freud sees some conflict between ego and id as inevitable, since the id is forever acting in accord with the pleasure principle, whilst the ego must also satisfy the dictates of a reality principle, and also, via the demands of the super-ego, a social-reality principle. It was the occasions when these conflicts got out of hand and over-flowed into experience and behaviour that primarily interested Freud as a clinician. He saw the neuroses as expressions of, and inadequate defences from, conflict-produced anxiety. Anxiety he identified as a response of the ego to uncontrollable levels of stimulation. Such uncontrollable stimulation might come from the external world, in which case Freud's model is indistinguishable from a learning theory point of view, such as Mowrer's (see Ch. 4); anxiety becomes attached to the imminence of a certain object or situation; by avoiding the situation in the face of the *signalling* anxiety the individual protects himself from whatever noxious stimulation he fears. However, Freud believed that overwhelming and uncontrollable stimulation does not always, or even usually, derive from real dangers; it can be the result of an excess of pressure from either id or super-ego impulses. The consequences of these threats is either neurotic anxiety or neurotic guilt. The anxiety experienced by the ego in both these cases, however, is still centred on the environment, since it is the effect of the impulses in causing loss, damage or disapproval that is feared. The difference between neurotic anxiety and real anxiety is that in the former case the ego is unconscious of the objects in the environment whose reactions are feared. Moreover, the unconsciously feared objects are not likely to be synonymous with the real objects, but are rather distortions resulting from prior associations with the same or similar objects.

This is an important consideration: psychoanalysts distinguish very clearly between *psychic reality* and *external reality*. As we noted when we talked about Lewin's ideas, he made a similar distinction between subjective and objective reality. We never have direct contact with external reality since we have to process our view of the world by the mechanisms of perception, and every psychologist of whatever persuasion accepts that motivational and personality factors influence perception. However perception can be more or less distorted, and what is more important, can suffer distortion at different levels. Thus a pound note for example, may at the conscious level be perceived as a pound note, and at the same time unconsciously awaken all sorts of associations and emotions which have very little connexion with a pound note: the pound note in this idiosyncratic world of psychic reality is an object perhaps with very different meanings for the individual. The objects which are feared in terms of neurotic anxiety dwell in this unconscious world of psychic reality, where money doesn't necessarily mean money but may mean faeces, where a father or later an authority figure may mean a castrator. Central to Freud's view of neurosis is that the adult has lost contact with this inner world and his conscious perceptions of his life situations seem normal. He is therefore unaware of the reasons for his seemingly unattached and free-floating anxiety. Nevertheless his responses of anxiety when these psychic objects are aroused or threatened by instinctual or super-ego demands continue, in the same way as do physiological reactions to a stimulus which is so subliminal that a person does not consciously perceive it. Perhaps it was to Freud's own detriment that he never expanded his thinking about this psychic reality world, peopled with distorted objects, shadows of the real people and objects in the external world. It was, however, an aspect of his theory which was taken up seriously by later disciples, in particular Melanie Klein.

But let us return to the ego which has to cope with neurotic anxiety. Unable through lack of insight to treat neurotic anxiety as effectively as it does anxiety from real dangers, the ego instead seeks more devious means. Such means can be generally classified under the heading of defence mechanisms.

Defence mechanisms

We have said that the ego has energy of its own, and the simplest way to get rid of unconsciously derived anxiety is to use that energy to push the anxiety firmly back where it belongs, in other words to operate a kind of mental avoidance response and deny its existence. Freud assumed that this mechanism of *repression* was used to banish all sorts of material which the ego could not tolerate in consciousness. However the operation of repression is not without its hazards. Originally we may suppose that the generation of anxiety was due to a fight between id impulses seeking expression and being repressed by the energies of the ego. As the fight required the use of more and more of the ego's supply of energy, so the symptoms of neurotic anxiety developed. It is easily appreciated that on such a model, further repression of the ensuing problems becomes less and less effective.

There are other methods, however, by which the ego may deal with the conflicts which generate anxiety. It can, for instance, project elements of the conflict on to other people. We are often aware of people doing this and we are apt to communicate our perspicacity by a statement of the sort: 'I think he doth protest too much'. Perhaps it is said of someone who is haranguing against ambition for riches: we may doubt his own behaviour if he were put in a position to realize such ambition. Another way of denying conflict is to reverse the unconscious aspects in consciousness. Hostility may be replaced by an over-concern for other people. This is known as reaction-formation: a good example is seen in Dickens's character of Uriah Heep – beneath the surface is a seething ambition, on the surface is an all too transparent humility. In the clinical patient, a fascination with anal eroticism and excreta may be translated into a consciously obsessive cleanliness.

These then are some of the methods the ego uses to defend itself. We shall see that the defence of the ego's integrity became even more important in post-Freudian theory.

Assessment of Freud's theory

There is no doubt that one reason why Freud's theories are still discussed in psychology is that they seem to do justice to the richness of an individual's experience in a way which seems lacking in other approaches to psychology. Nevertheless there are criticisms which have to be made and these criticisms are very similar to those made of the early ethologists (see Ch. 2). Freud's is an energy model. Forces are postulated which build up until the energy has to spill out in some way, or be dammed up, or channelled. Moreover the forces are all inside the organism, and there is scant attention in orthodox psychoanalytic theory to the environment and the capacity for external stimuli to control and govern behaviour. As for the raw observations made by Freud, it is largely a matter of personal preference how much credence one puts on them, but it is clear that they do not have as much universality as Freud perhaps originally thought. The classic Oedipus complex is likely to be seen only in certain kinds of family-structured societies. However, various experimental findings have been shown to support certain of Freud's ideas, and the interested reader is referred to Kline (1972) for further details.

On the general issue of unconscious motivation, Freud should not be faulted. True, his energy model of anxiety and conflict being aroused by id urges is not exactly fashionable. However, it is possible to see that *external* stimuli can come to elicit anxiety. Stimuli perceived as *similar* will also elicit anxiety by the principle of generalization (see Ch. 4). Now it is known from laboratory experiments that similarity can be judged on semantic grounds – thus a conditioned response to the word SEA will also be elicited by the word WAVE, more than by an obviously more physically similar word such as SEE (see A6). The semantic relationships which exist in the mind of a young child would probably allow anxiety to be generated by a process of generalization in the presence of all sorts of apparently innocuous stimuli. To the extent that a person may not be aware of the childhood associations which are evoked by everyday stimuli, we can well imagine a person suffering free-floating anxiety, apparently unattached to real threats in the external world. In short, we can admit that the world we see gives rise to our conscious perceptions, it also translates itself into a world of unconscious associations.

Post-Freudian developments in psychoanalysis

One of the main movements in psychoanalytic thinking since Freud has been in the direction of giving the ego more of a central place on stage. Melanie Klein trained as a Freudian analyst and then worked with very young children. She placed much more emphasis than Freud on the aggressive impulses of the young child rather than on libidinal impulses. In particular she sought to show how the young baby perceives the world and how the self which develops continues to colour its relationships with the adult world according to its very earliest experiences. She defined two *positions* which the baby psychologically adopts: the *paranoid/schizoid position*, and the *depressive position*. The baby at first is thought of as unable to differentiate real objects; instead *sensations* are objects. Thus the breast or the mother is split into a 'good mother' and a 'bad mother'. The baby supposedly reacts to the bad mother with intense persecutory feelings of anger and entertains phantasies of the most murderous kind (usually involving both devouring and spitting out and generally oral activity – since the world of sensations at this time supposedly centres on the mouth). The baby is alternatively omnipotent and schizoid (in the presence of the good mother) or overwhelmed and threatened with persecutory anxiety (in the presence or feared presence of the bad mother). This, then, is the paranoid/schizoid position. As the child becomes more realistic it can no longer split the same object. It has to accept that the object it loved is the same as the object it hated and this gives rise to the 'depressive' position. If the child has not been flooded with too much persecutory anxiety (from either environmental causes or an over-active death instinct) it is able to make reparations and acquire a self which can genuinely relate with other persons, recognized as different and integral in their own right. However Klein believed that in many cases, and probably in all of us from time to time, there is an inability to tolerate the depressive position, because persecutory anxiety has been too intense. The individual then regresses to the paranoid/schizoid position.

Klein's views about the earliest world of the young baby reach the very heights of speculation. However we have mentioned her theory in detail here because of all classic psychoanalytic thinkers she is probably the key to subsequent developments, which take us even out of the field of psychoanalysis. The 'positions' which she speaks of are to be seen as the two fundamental ways a person can *be in the world.* The paranoid/schizoid position describes an ego which feels so threatened that it cuts itself off from true relationships with other persons and retreats into a false omnipotence (the schizoid feature); relationships with the world cannot be severed entirely so communication is made possible by the development of a facade which mediates more or less successfully with a basically hostile and threatening world of other people.

Although Klein never says so, she comes close to recognizing an ego at birth rather than an id. Later analysts, notably Fairbairn (1952), have openly altered Freud's own structures and postulated solely an ego, which itself becomes fragmented. He speaks of a *libidinal ego,* the core of the self, and a *central ego.* In terms of Klein's positions, it is the central ego which keeps up a facade, whilst the libidinal ego retreats into an impregnable fortress. Alternatively if the depressive position is tolerated and overcome, no great split will develop within the ego itself.

Lest the reader should feel that motivation has been lost in this discussion, it should be stressed that it has not! The very important point, implicit in this development, is that there is one need which overshadows all others: that one should have a self which feels secure. The problems, complexes, and conflicts that Freud described are still seen as real but they are seen in the light ultimately of an already damaged sense of identity, a weakened ego.

This naturally has had a profound effect on the practice of psychoanalysis. Instead of the aim being solely that of gaining insight into the unconscious source of problems, the aim is rather to provide a therapeutic relationship in which the patient may find contact with his real self. Contemporary analysts, such as Guntrip (1968), talk of locating the 'child within' – pointing to the fact that many patients' problems stem from their denial of a weak but very real self and hiding it behind an adult and strong facade. In so far as this leads to feelings of 'not being a real person' (derealization) the defence is inadequate and the patient seeks help.

Although many (perhaps most) analysts remain more orthodox, the sort of development we have been discussing can be seen in those who would call themselves still basic Freudians. Thus Winnicott (1965) speaks not of a 'child within' but a self which is put into storage – a very similar concept.

Lastly we should mention R. D. Laing (1965). He, too, sees the fundamental problem as one of false self, apparently successfully coping with reality but stifling a real self, which lies behind the facade.

All these thinkers differ from Freud in one very important respect. Freud's pessimism never allowed him truly to formulate what he meant by 'health'. He knew only mental sickness, and mental health really was just its absence. We now discover, in these later analysts, a more powerful motive than libidinal impulses, and a more positive goal than absence of psychopathology: the motive is to discover and be the self which one truly is. There is an American psychologist, not a psychoanalyst, who came to a similar conclusion. His name is Carl Rogers. Like the contemporary analysts mentioned, his main focus has been on the existential question of 'being-for-oneself' (true self) or 'being-for-others' (false self).

Rogers (1967) outlines various goals which he feels an individual needs to strive for (see D3 and F1). Although he has never subscribed to the psychoanalytic school of thinking, he too developed his ideas in a therapeutic context of treating patients. Among the goals he points to are 'positive self regard' and 'being one's own organism'. The two goals are of course inter-related: patients are usually afraid to be their own organism (or the self which they truly are – another of Roger's phrases) because they do not regard it as positive or strong, but as shameful and weak.

The task of therapy is to foster self-growth and Rogers has always placed the whole of his therapeutic emphasis on establishing the right relationship with clients, and engaging in the minimum of interpretation of patient's statements (unlike orthodox analysis). The typical Rogerian therapist tries rather to mirror his clients verbalizations and thus convey the fact that he understands, or at least is trying very hard to understand. Rogers maintains that it is the qualities that the therapist brings to the relationship which enhance or interfere with the natural tendency towards self-growth. The Rogerians have in fact established a reputable catalogue of research findings which point to the importance of three qualities in the therapist which are of extreme benefit to clients. They are: empathy, warmth and genuineness (see Truax and Carkhuff, 1967). More recently Rogers has become increasingly interested in group experiences as facilitating the achievement of the goals with which he has been concerned. His experience with 'encounter' groups (Rogers, 1973) has led to his inclusion in the list of so called humanistic psychologists. We end with a short account of the humanistic movement.

Humanistic psychology is really an umbrella term to describe an approach to psychology, shared by a number of contemporary psychologists, who feel that the traditional conception of man, as he has been studied scientifically, has been misguided (see F1, F7 and F8). They assert that man is not reducible to his physiology, neither is he a mechanistic or even cognitive responder to stimuli, neither, finally, is he a battleground for sexual and aggressive impulses. Although these approaches can illuminate partially man's behaviour, they all ignore what is given to us at first hand – that we are and feel ourselves to be persons. Now persons can feel more or less real, more or less fulfilled, more or less in relationship to one another. The danger of traditional conceptions of man is, according to humanistic psychologists, the very fact that these conceptions themselves help to determine the way we see ourselves, the way we feel, and ultimately (because they overlook the ultimate motive towards genuine personalization) help to create the depersonalization, derealization and general alienation which we see around us. Put succinctly, we may say that to see man at second hand through his behaviour rather than through his experience is ultimately to see ourselves at second hand and never *be* ourselves.

Maslow (1959), who is one of the key precursors of humanistic psychology, puts forward a number of motives in the form of a hierarchy. Without disputing many of the motives we have discussed in this book, he would however add, at the top of the hierarchy, the motive towards *self-actualization*. It is clear from Maslow's description of the self-actualized person that his conception is very similar to Rogers' of becoming more and more the organism that one is.

There are a lot of assumptions about human nature implicit in the concepts used by humanistic psychologists and it is too early to judge the movement. However it is a promising development in modern psychology for two reasons. First, as we have seen, it is an optimistic movement. The basic nature of man, when he is freed from his defensive falsitudes, is assumed to be not wild and uncontrollable (as feared by Freud) but positive, loving and sociable (Rogers, 1967). Secondly, just because the phenomena, the experiences and assumed personal changes happen in circumstances such as encounter groups, sensitivity groups or whatever, does not mean that scientific support cannot be obtained (Rogers, 1973). Psychologists are only now becoming used to the idea that one can get useful and scientific data by asking people how they are experiencing the world around them.

Summary

1 Freud's ideas about the determinants of man's behaviour about unconscious motivation, and about instinctual impulses are outlined, in the context of their historical development.
2 Freud's dynamic instinctual model is criticized. However some of his views have experimental support, and the idea of unconscious motivation in principle is not objectionable.
3 Later analysts have placed more emphasis on the ego. In particular they have stressed that the ego needs above all to feel safe and unthreatened. A false safety is often secured by severing all connexions with the real self, and building up a false facade. This strategy ultimately fails because it is assumed that there are powerful motives for a self to become realized in relationship to others.
4 The same over-riding motives towards real self, being-for-oneself, being one's own organism, self-actualization, etc., have been given prominence in America by psycho-

logists such as Rogers and Maslow. Recently similar thinkers have banded together under the banner of 'humanistic psychology'. Their aim is to demonstrate the truth of their position by methods of direct experience, including encounter and sensitivity training groups.

7
Codetta

And now the summing up. Not 'what do we mean by motivation?' rather, 'what have we meant?' The main emphasis of the book has been to answer the former question by looking for factors which control behaviour. We started by looking at behaviour which is controlled in as simple a way as possible. We looked at instinct and saw the existence of relatively fixed behaviour patterns, seemingly innately laid down in an organism's physical make-up. We criticized some of the formulations of ethologists, not because their observations have been faulty, nor even because we disagreed with the idea of innate fixed patterns of behaviour. Rather we criticized the approach which seemed to beg the question of innateness, and of behavioural rigidity before experimentation and observation. We argued that this restricted research rather than expanded it.

Other behaviours such as eating, drinking, sexual activity, and sleeping were also seen as having bases of control at the simple neuro-physiological level. But even these cannot be considered independently of the environmental stimuli which arouse the organism. We saw the importance of environmental stimuli, particularly in the case of sexual activity in higher animals.

We then moved on to a consideration of the control of acquired behaviour in general. The mechanistic system of Hull maintained the idea of control from within the organism, in the form of a unitary drive force, which derived from the frustration of basic physiological needs. The drive concept proved extremely productive for the psychology of motivation, but ultimately discovered its limitations with the emergence of incentive factors. The incentive or reinforcement at the end of behavioural sequences seemed enough to explain why an organism performs responses.

The idea that external stimuli are the controlling feature of behaviour led us to ask the question of how the organism, particularly the human organism, processes those stimuli. Early cognitive theorists, reaching right through to people like Atkinson, never went much further in their invocation of cognition than to postulate 'expectations'. A system such as Atkinson's, though it dealt with peculiarly human motives and goals, still saw performance to be a function of traditional type variables: a motive, an expectation, and a reinforcement. It was left to social psychologists such as Schachter, Festinger and others, to show how the cognition of these variables is amenable to manipulation, prior to the cognition affecting behaviour.

Freudian notions of motivation are both within and without the traditional development, which we have so far traced. They are within in the sense that Freud was a determinist and sought to show how behaviour was in fact controlled. He was outside the tradition in so far as he conceived of fundamental motivation as being unconscious, and due, in the main, to sexual and aggressive impulses.

Post-Freudian developments take us right out of the tradition, implicit in the rest of the book. We are asked to move from one philosophical perspective (roughly called empiricism) to a completely different one (roughly called existentialism). There is one thing we do not have to prove (by empirical enquiry) and that is that we *are* – the subjunctive we *be* might be a better way of putting it. If it is true that we *be*, so it is true that *we* be. The concept of self is logically prior to everything. (This is not solely the view of existentially inclined thinkers, but reflects developments in linguistic philosophy – see Strawson, 1965; and F7.) The motive to be the self that one truly is achieves prominence in the views of 'humanistic' psychologists.

Future developments

First, the area of cognition in motivation will necessarily expand. Research into the effects of modifying cognitions, whether it be for experimental or therapeutic reasons, is likely to increase. If one looks at behaviour modification procedures as they have developed in clinical practice (see F3), one sees very clearly in recent years a shift away from looking for a simple target response to 'cure'; instead there has been a move towards close (but still objective) analyses of how the patient's superficial symptoms reflect more general ways of coping (or failing to cope) with his environment (Evans and Liggett, 1971). Anxiety or fear, as a motive to avoid, is particularly in the melting pot at the moment. No longer are modification procedures seen as extinguishing the fear response in any simple way (Wolpe, 1958); instead modification when it is successful probably involves changes of cognition, leading to coping behaviour (Meichenbaum, 1971; Goldfried, 1971).

Lastly in the field of encounter groups and sensitivity training, research findings relating to outcome are likely to mushroom (see Smith, 1974) and thus make it possible to assess better the status of seemingly crucial but hazy motives such as self-actualization, and the like.

As far as human motivation is concerned, the one certainty is that the 'person' is back in psychology. The days of a psychology of the empty organism are gone.

References and Name Index

The numbers in italics after each entry refer to page numbers within this book.

Andersson, B. (1953) The effect of injections of hypertonic NaCl solutions into different parts of the hypothalamus of goats. *Acta Physiologica Scandinavica 28*: 188–201. *49*

Andersson, B. and Larssen, S. (1961) Influence of local temperature changes in the pre-optic and rostral hypothalamus on the regulation of food and water intake. *Acta Physiologica Scandinavica 52*: 75–89. *43*

Aronson, E. and Carlsmith, J. M. (1963) Effects of severity of threat on the deviation of forbidden behaviour. *Journal of Abnormal and Social Psychology 66*: 584–8. *102*

Atkinson, J. W. and Litwin, G. H. (1960) Achievement motive and test anxiety, conceived as a motive to approach success and to avoid failure. *Journal of Abnormal and Social Psychology 60*: 52–63. *95*

Bandura, A. (1969) *Principles of Behaviour Modification.* Holt, Rinehart and Winston. *102*

Beach, F. A. and Jordan, L. (1956) Effect of sexual exhaustion and recovery in the male rat. *Quarterly Journal of Experimental Psychology 8*: 121–33. *58*

Bellows, R. T. and Van Wagenen, W. P. (1939) The effects of resection of the olfactory, gustatory and trigeminal nerves on water drinking in dogs, with and without diabetes insipidus. *American Journal of Physiology 126*: 13–19. *47*

Bindra, D. (1969) The inter-related mechanism of reinforcement and motivation, and the nature of their influence on response. *Nebraska Symposium on Motivation 17*: 1–38. *80*

Birch, D., Burnstein, E. and Clark, R. A. (1958) Response strength as a function of food deprivation under a controlled maintenance schedule. *Journal of Comparative & Physiological Psychology 51*: 350–4. *79*

Bowlby, J. (1969) *Attachment and Loss.* London: Hogarth Press. *30*

Brehm, J. W. (1962) Motivational aspects of cognitive dissonance. *Nebraska Symposium on Motivation 10*: 51–77. *102*

Brobeck, J. R. (1955) Neural regulation of food intake. *Annals of the New York Academy of Science 63*: 44–55. *43*

Brown, J. S. (1953) Problem presented by the concept of acquired drives. Reproduced in D. Bindra and J. Stewart (eds) *Motivation.* Harmondsworth: Penguin, 1966. *69, 78*

Bugelski, B. R. (1938) Extinction with and without sub-goal reinforcement. *Journal of Comparative Psychology 26*: 121–33. *65*

Cowles, J. T. (1937) Food tokens as incentives for learning by chimpanzees. *Comparative Psychology Monograph 14* (Series 7). *66, 69*

Crespi, L. P. (1942) Quantitative variation of incentive and performance in the white rat. *American Journal of Psychology 55*: 467–517. *78*

Duner, H. (1953) The influence of blood glucose level on the secretion of adrenalin and noradrenalin from the suprarenal. *Acta Physiologica Scandinavica 28,* Suppl. 102: 77. *42*

Dunham, P. J. (1971) Punishment. *Psychological Review 78*: 58. *68*

Epstein, A. N. (1971) In E. Stellar and J. M. Sprague (eds) *Progress in Physiological Psychology, 4.* New York: Academic Press. *45*

Evans, P. D. and Liggett, J. (1971) Loss and bereavement as factors in agoraphobia: implications for therapy. *British Journal of Medical Psychology 44*: 149–54. *132*

Fairbairn, W. R. D. (1952) *Psychoanalytic Studies of the Personality*. London: Tavistock. *124*

Feather, N. T. (1961) The relationship of persistence at a task to expectation of success and achievement related motives. *Journal of Abnormal and Social Psychology 63*: 552–61. *95*

Festinger, L. and Carlsmith, J. M. (1959) Cognitive consequences of forced compliance. *Journal of Abnormal and Social Psychology 58*: 203–10. *101*

Fitzsimons, J. T. (1971) In E. Stellar and J. M. Sprague (eds) *Progress in Physiological Psychology, 4*. New York: Academic Press. *49*

Ford, C. S. and Beach, F. A. (1951) *Patterns of Sexual Behaviour*. New York: Harper. *57*

French, E. G. and Thomas, F. (1958) The relation of achievement motivation to problem-solving effectiveness. *Journal of Abnormal and Social Psychology 56*: 45–8. *92*

Goldfried, H. Systematic desensitization as training in self-control. *Journal of Consulting & Clinical Psychology 37*: 228. *132*

Gray, J. and Smith, P. T. (1969) In R. M. Gilbert and N. J. Sutherland (eds) *Animal Discrimination Learning*. London: Academic Press. *71*

Green, M., Green, R. and Carr, W. J. (1966) The hawk-goose phenomenon: a replication and an extension. *Psychonomic Science 4*: 185–6. *33*

Green, R., Carr, W. J. and Green, M. (1968) The hawk-goose phenomenon: Further confirmation and a search for the releases. *Journal of Psychology 69*: 271–6. *33*

Grossman, M. I., Cummins, G. M. and Ivy, A. C. (1947). The effect of insulin on food intake after vagotomy and sympathectomy. *American Journal of Physiology 1*: 263–9. *38*

Guntrip, H. (1964) *Healing the Sick Mind*. London: Unwin Books. *113*

Guntrip, H. (1968) *Schizoid Phenomena, Object-relations, and the Self*. London: Hogarth Press. *125*

Hinde, R. (1970) *Animal Behaviour: A Synthesis of Ethology and Comparative Psychology*. Holt, Rinehart and Winston. *35*

Jouvet, M. (1967) The sleeping brain. *Science Journal*, May

1967 (special issue). *54*

Keehn, J. D. (1969) In R. M. Gilbert and N. S. Sutherland (eds) *Animal Discrimination Learning*. New York: Academic Press. *81*

Kendler, H. H. (1945) Drive interaction: I. Learning as a function of the simultaneous presence of the hunger and thirst drives. *Journal of Experimental Psychology 35*: 96–109. *71*

Kinsey, A. C., Pomeroy, W. B. and Martin, C. E. (1948) *Sexual Behaviour in the Human Male*. Philadelphia: W. B. Saunders. *56, 59, 60*

Kinsey, A. C., Pomeroy, W. B., Martin, C. A. and Gebhard, P. H. (1952) *Sexual Behaviour in the Human Female*. Philadelphia: W. B. Saunders. *59, 60*

Kline, P. (1972) *Fact and Fantasy in Freudian Theory*. London: Methuen. *122*

Kohler, W. (1925) *The Mentality of Apes*. New York: Harcourt Brace. *87*

Laing, R. D. (1965) *The Divided Self*. Harmondsworth: Pelican Books. *125*

Lang, P. J. (1968) Fear reduction and fear behaviour: problems in treating a construct. *Research in Psychotherapy 3*: 90–102. *100*

Lazarus, R. S. and Opton, E. M. (Jr) (1966) In C. D. Spielberger (ed.) *Anxiety and Behaviour*. New York: Academic Press. *100*

Lazarus, R. S. (1968) Emotion and adaptation: conceptual and empirical relations. *Nebraska Symposium on Motivation 66*: 175–270. *100*

Lorenz, K. (1950) The comparative method of studying innate behaviour patterns. Symposium of Society for Experimental Biology. Cambridge: C.U.P. *29, 34*

Lowell, E. L. (1952) The effect of need for achievement on learning and speed of performance. *Journal of Psychology 33*: 31–40. *91*

Mahone, C. (1960) Fear of failure in unrealistic vocational aspirations. *Journal of Abnormal and Social Psychology 60*: 253–61. *96*

Maslow, A. H. (1959) Cognition of being in the peak experiences. *Journal of Genetic Psychology 94*: 43–66. *127*

Mayer, J. and Greenberg, R. M. (1953) Hyperthermia in

hypothalamic hyperphagia. *American Journal of Physiology 173*: 523–5. *44*

Mayer, J. (1955) Regulation of energy intake and the body weight: the glucostatic theory and the lipostatic hypothesis. *Annals of the New York Academy of Science 63*, 1: 15–43. *41*

Mayer, J. and Barnett, R. J. (1955) Obesity following unilateral hypothalamic lesions in rats. *Science 121*: 599. *40*

Meichenbaum, D. M. (1971) Examination of model characteristics in reducing avoidance behaviour. *Journal of Personality and Social Psychology 17*: 298–307. *132*

Mendelson, J. (1966) Role of hunger in T-maze learning for food by rats. *Journal of Comparative and Physiological Psychology 62*: 341–9. *80*

Meryman, J. J. (1952) Magnitude of startle response as a function of hunger and fear. Unpublished Master's Thesis, University of Iowa. *71*

McClelland, D. C., Atkinson, J. W., Clark, R. W. and Lowell, E. L. (1953) *The Achievement Motive*. New York: Appleton-Century-Crofts. *91*

McClelland, D. C. (1961) *The Achieving Society*. Princeton, N.J.: Van Nostrand. *92*

McClelland, D. C. and Winter, D. G. (1969) *Motivating Economic Achievement*. New York: Free Press. *92*

Miller, N. E. (1948) Studies of fear as an acquirable drive. *Journal of Experimental Psychology 38*: 89–101. *67*

Mischel, W. (1961) Delay of gratification, need for achievement, and acquiescence in another culture. *Journal of Abnormal and Social Psychology 62*: 543–52. *92*

Montgomery, H. P. (1931) The influence of atropine and pilocarpine on thirst. *American Journal of Physiology 98*: 35–41. *47*

Moruzzi, G. (1964) Reticular influences in the E.E.G. *Electroencephology and Clinical Neurophysiology 16*: 2–17. *53*

Olds, J. and Milner, P. (1954) Positive reinforcement produced by electrical stimulation of septal area and other regions of rat brain. *Journal of Comparative & Physiological Psychology 47*: 419–27. *82*

Oswald, I. (1966) *Sleep*. Harmondsworth: Penguin. *51*

Richter, C. P. (1927) Animal behaviour and internal drives.

Quarterly Review of Biology 2: 307–43. *45*
Richter, C. P. (1942) Total self regulatory functions in animals and human beings. *Harvey Lectures 38*: 63–103. *45*
Rogers, C. (1967) *On Becoming a Person*. London: Constable. *126, 128*
Rogers, C. (1973) *Encounter Groups*. Harmondsworth: Penguin. *126, 128*
Schachter, S. and Singer, J. E. (1962) Cognitive, social and physiological determinants of emotional state. *Psychological Review 69*: 379–99. *98*
Schneirla, P. C. (1965) Aspects of stimulus and organization in approach/withdrawal process underlying vertebrate behavioural development. *Advanced Studies in Behaviour 1*: 1–71. *32*
Sheffield, F. D., Wulff, J. T. and Baker, R. (1951) Reward value of copulation without sex drive reduction. *Journal of Comparative and Physiological Psychology 44*: 3–8. *82*
Smith, P. (1974) Controlled studies of outcome of sensitivity training. Mimeograph. University of Sussex. *132*
Strawson, P. F. (1965) *Individuals: An Essay in Descriptive Metaphysics*. London: Methuen. *132*
Stunckard, A. J. (1957) Studies in the physiology of hunger. *American Journal of Clinical Nutrition 5*, 203–11. *42, 44*
Stunckard, A. J., Van Itallian, T. B. and Reiss, B. B. (1955) The mechanism of satiety: the effect of glucagon on gastric hunger contractions in man. *Proceedings of the Society of Experimental Biology and Medicine 89*: 258–61. *42*
Teitelbaum, P. and Epstein, A. N. (1962) The lateral hypothalamic syndrome: recovery of feeding and drinking after lateral hypothalamic lesions. *Psychological Review 69*: 74–90. *40*
Tinbergen, N. (1951) *The Study of Instinct*. Oxford: O.U.P. *26, 32*
Tolman, E. C. and Honzig, C. H. (1930) Introduction and renewal of reward and maze performance in rats. *Berkeley, University of California Publications in Psychology 4* (19): 267. *77*
Truax, C. B. and Carkhuff, R. R. (1967) *Towards Effective Counselling and Psychotherapy*. Chicago: Aldine. *126*
Valins, S. (1966) Cognitive effects of false heart-rate feedback.

Journal of Personality and Social Psychology 4: 400–8. *99*
Valins, S. and Ray, A. A. (1967) Effects of cognitive dissonance on avoidance behaviour. *Journal of Personality and Social Psychology* 7: 345–50. *99*
Verney, E. B. (1947) The A.D.H. and the factors which determine its release. *Proceedings of the Royal Society, London 135*: 25–106. *48*
Windsor, A. L. (1930) The effect of dehydration on parotid secretion. *American Journal of Psychology* 42: 602–7. *47*
Wolpe, J. (1958) *Psychotherapy by Reciprocal Inhibition.* Stanford: Stanford University Press. *132*

Subject Index